FREEING THE SPIRIT

FREEING
THE SPIRIT

The Iconic
Women
of Modern India

Edited by
MALVIKA SINGH

PENGUIN BOOKS

PENGUIN BOOKS
Published by the Penguin Group
Penguin Books India Pvt. Ltd, 11 Community Centre, Panchsheel Park,
New Delhi 110 017, India
Penguin Group (USA) Inc., 375 Hudson Street, New York, New York 10014,
USA
Penguin Group (Canada), 90 Eglinton Avenue East, Suite 700, Toronto,
Ontario, Canada M4P 2Y3 (a division of Pearson Penguin Canada Inc.)
Penguin Books Ltd, 80 Strand, London WC2R 0RL, England
Penguin Ireland, 25 St Stephen's Green, Dublin 2, Ireland (a division of
Penguin Books Ltd)
Penguin Group (Australia), 250 Camberwell Road, Camberwell, Victoria
3124, Australia (a division of Pearson Australia Group Pty Ltd)
Penguin Group (NZ), cnr Airborne and Rosedale Roads, Albany, Auckland
1310, New Zealand (a division of Pearson New Zealand Ltd)
Penguin Group (South Africa) (Pty) Ltd, 24 Sturdee Avenue, Rosebank,
Johannesburg 2196, South Africa

Penguin Books Ltd, Registered Offices: 80 Strand, London WC2R 0RL,
England

First published by Penguin Books India 2006

Anthology copyright © Penguin Books India 2006
Introduction copyright © Malvika Singh 2006
The copyright for individual pieces vests with the authors or their estates

10 9 8 7 6 5 4 3 2 1

ISBN-13: 978-0-14310-082-9   ISBN-10: 0-14310-082-3

For sale in the Indian Subcontinent only

Typeset in Sabon by Mantra Virtual Services, New Delhi
Printed at Chaman Offset Printers, New Delhi

For Anjali and her creative spirit.

Contents

INTRODUCTION ix

HAI AKHTARI! 1
S. Kalidas on Begum Akhtar

WHY NARGIS MATTERS 14
T.J.S. George on Nargis

A LIFE IN SERVICE 28
Subhashini Ali Sahgal on Lakshmi Sahgal

BREAKING THE STATUS QUO 47
Shikha Trivedy on Mayawati

REVIVAL AND RESTORATION 63
Jaya Jaitly on Kamaladevi Chattopadhyay

AMMA: THE ENIGMA 83
*Sushila Ravindranath on
J. Jayalalithaa*

THE TAPESTRY OF HER LIFE 94
Malvika Singh on Pupul Jayakar

UPPING THE ANTE   103
Naazneen Karmali on Kiran Mazumdar-Shaw

THE MIRACLE MOTHER 113
Reeta Devi on Mother Teresa

A RICH CANVAS   122
Nitin Bhayana on Amrita Sher-Gil

CONQUERING THE SCALE   132
Bhawana Somaaya on Lata Mangeshkar

ARCHIVING THE NATION   145
Sabeena Gadihoke on Homai Vyarawalla

CELEBRATING EXCELLENCE   152
Leela Samson on Rukmini Devi Arundale

THE ADIVASI MAHASVETA   166
Ganesh N. Devy on Mahasveta Devi

THE ASCENT OF THE
ORDINARY   177
Tarun J. Tejpal on Sonia Gandhi

LOOKING FOR INDIRA
GANDHI   195
Sunil Khilnani on Indira Gandhi

NOTES ON CONTRIBUTORS   214
ACKNOWLEDGEMENTS   216

Introduction

This anthology tells the stories of women who arrived at the pinnacles of their professions, stood by their beliefs, struggled, endured extreme stress and were constantly faced with complex realities, but displayed exterior calm and an amazing ability to survive just about anything. It is these qualities that have been the inner fortitude and backbone of womankind. Here, we have a small representation of women, by no means all-encompassing. Some have passed on, leaving behind a wealth of experience and a vibrant, living legacy, having initiated movements that were larger than themselves. Others continue to create and break new ground, adjusting with astonishing ease into a relentlessly changing world. In essence, this is a living anthology.

I have had the honour and privilege of knowing some of these women personally, and so have many of the contributors who have written for this collection. I hope the reader will get to see a more intimate side to these personalities. The story of a woman's life cannot be demarcated into the 'private' and the 'public'; the black and the white. The private and the public are interdependent—one motivates the other in subtle and unexpected ways.

In a world torn apart by strife, surrounded by poverty of the mind and soul, devoid of tolerance, compassion and respect, a young girl from the Macedonian town of Skopje went on to be known as Mother Teresa. She spoke of love—

simple, straightforward love—that should be immanent in us all. Capable of being strong and gentle at the same time, when she looked at you it was as if her eyes could pierce through all the protective trappings we tend to hide behind. I personally experienced this somewhat unnerving quality in her. When I met her in 1994, she looked at me with a sharp and focused stare and asked me whether I believed in God. Being an agnostic, confused and unsure about such things, I said that I was not sure whether I did or didn't.

Did I believe in the power of prayer, then? A bit put out, I once again said that I was not sure of that either. Sensing my embarrassment, she put her arms around me and told me I was a good woman, and that obviously my work was my prayer. She then suddenly asked me what was weighing on my mind. I was surprised by the directness of her question, but opened up to her immediately. I told her about Kim Housego, the son of my friends David and Jenny Housego, who had been kidnapped by militants in Kashmir while the family was holidaying in Pahalgam. It had been nearly two weeks with no information but for endless unsubstantiated rumours, and hope was fading. She held my hands in hers and said she would pray all night in the chapel with the Sisters of Charity. She would prove the power of prayer. Bewildered, and naturally a bit sceptical, I went home.

The next evening, as I was about to leave my office, I had a call from a friend who said that rumours were flying about Kim's release, but no one knew anything for sure. When I got home I had a phone call from Mother: 'Mala, Kim has been set free by the militants. Will you now believe in the power of prayer?' That experience changed the way I look at the world and at the unknown.

Reeta Devi writes about Mother Teresa and their

relationship, which was built over years of working together. Reeta too embodies the gift of giving unconditionally. She works with the poor and the destitute, with sex workers, AIDS patients and drug addicts, helping them out of their despair.

In sharp contrast was the artist Amrita Sher-Gil, who died young but lived a full life through her twenty-eight years. She had been there and seen it all. A child of two cultures, she finally put down her roots in India, having lived between Paris, Hungary and this country. Evoking unforgettable images of rural India with a colour palette that was earthy, sensuous and rich, Amrita's Sikh and Hungarian cultural patterns influenced her life and work through the mood and style of her paintings. She too broke out of the restrictive confines of her time and class, liberated herself from conservative social mores, and followed her heart.

Nitin Bhayana, a collector of contemporary Indian art who started to pursue his passion as a young man, writes about Amrita Sher-Gil. He has also spent time with the painter F.N. Souza in New York when he was a student, and has built a splendid collection of the artist's drawings.

Then there was Rukmini Devi Arundale, the creator of Kalakshetra, an institution that has withstood the changing mores of changing times. Kalakshetra has produced some of India's greatest classical dancers. It has a long and deserved reputation as a place of learning which uses the best traditional teaching methods while incorporating contemporary influences in dance. Rukmini Devi's student Leela Samson is today at the helm of this institution, carrying forward the tradition envisioned by its founder. She, as a shishya, tells the story of her guru.

Begum Akhtar, hypnotized by her own music, broke loose from the rigidities of the prevailing cultural constraints and her conservative social environment. With her transcendental voice she enthralled not only her own generation but several that followed, traversing a difficult path. Her cameo in Satyajit Ray's poignant film, *Jalsaghar*, remains an indelible visual in the minds of those who saw it. S. Kalidas, a lifelong devotee of Begum Akhtar, made a documentary on her life and music, spending years buried in research and meeting the people who knew her best. He brings his experiences to this anthology.

Nargis was the embodiment of a graciousness that was rare in her time, but is a near mirage today. Her stunning appearance, acting prowess and popularity did not shield her from the social conservatism of her time, but her inner dignity and resilience gave her strength. Nargis was a pioneer who set the parameters for future actresses, establishing the respectability the profession enjoys today. T.J.S. George, a journalist by profession, has written a comprehensive account of the life and times of Nargis.

Homai Vyarawalla always looked ahead. As she captured her time and contemporaries on still film, she established the ground for professional photography in India. Even at the start of the new millennium, to be a dedicated photographer is a struggle, as the profession does not get the credence and respect it deserves. When India integrates with the international scene and the prices of photographs are determined by the international standard, photographers will be accepted as artists soon enough. Homai, therefore, must be celebrated, albeit half a century later, for sticking to her guns. Sabeena Gadihoke, who has put together a book on Homai Vyarawalla's work, has written for this collection of essays.

In my youth I would be jeered for wearing handloom saris instead of bell-bottom pants and frilly skirts. The same women who taunted me, now middle-aged, are now out there buying Venkatgiris, Tangails, Upadas and pure khadi, having forgotten their not too distant past! Pupul Jayakar and Kamaladevi Chattopadhyay understood Indian arts and crafts, and will be remembered for having stirred and revived the latent 'legacy industries', considered to be one of India's most valuable human resources. Both these women, who had a mandate from independent India's first government to rejuvenate and restructure this enormous economic sector, were my mentors. With the understanding, support and unconditional backing given by Indira Gandhi, India's traditional knowledge-based industries live on, generating wealth and providing employment to millions of people. Jaya Jaitly, who knew and worked with Kamaladevi, is the initiator and driving force of the successful Dilli Haat experiment. She has also put together a series of maps that show the distribution of local crafts and skills across India. In this collection, she writes about the woman who inspired her.

Kiran Mazumdar-Shaw, the new generation leader of India's knowledge industries, competed in a male-dominated environment and made her presence felt, unobtrusively and with firm conviction. Hers is a classic example of unflinching female determination laced with elegance. She has laid the foundation for a whole new avenue of growth in this country, proving that men and women share the same domains and are equals. She is a rare breed: a first-generation businesswoman; a creator, not an inheritor. An account of her success has been written by Naazneen Karmali, who writes on the corporate world and has followed the career graph of Kiran Mazumdar-Shaw with a meticulous eye.

Mahasveta Devi is a living treasure. She lives her work, and has devoted all her physical and mental energies to tribal communities. She has shared her life with the less privileged, extending her mind and soul to them, working to make them feel a part of the larger Indian community. Literature and humanity are two arms of the same body, and Mahasveta Devi is a rare, living example of their union. Ganesh N. Devy, who also works with tribal communities, takes us on a journey with Mahasveta Devi, revealing the intense story of her life.

I have known Lakshmi Sahgal for half my life, and she remains just as energetic, curious and on the ball as she was when I first met her. Lakshmi Sahgal only looks ahead—no grumbling, no regrets. A remarkable fighter, she has always been ready to protest against injustice. Her values are set in stone, unwavering, giving her the supreme confidence she exudes. Her once firebrand daughter, Subhashini Ali Sahgal, a proverbial chip off the old block, has written this charming and personal tribute to her mother, mentor and guide.

Lata Mangeshkar has conquered India like few have been able to. North or South, East or West, whether or not you understand Hindi, whatever music tradition you are from, as long as you are Indian it is very likely that Lata Mangeshkar and her voice have made an impact on you in some way. Her rise has been unstoppable, with no dip in the scale at all, an almost unimaginable feat. Her voice and music have impacted everyone, regardless of community, caste, creed, or age. Her biographer here is Bhawana Somaaya, who has been writing about the film industry for years, and is among the best film critics of our time.

And finally, the political women of India. J. Jayalalithaa operates like a Queen Empress in Tamil Nadu—whether or not she is in power is incidental. She leaves no stone unturned to achieve what she wants. Her charismatic appeal has effectively overwhelmed her electorate. Educated and urbane, no one doubts that she is a mass leader to contend with.

Jayalalithaa has remained inaccessible, an enigma. Sushila Ravindranath, the editor of the *Sunday Express*, grew up with Jayalalithaa. She shares her insights with us in this collection.

Detached, distant and clear about her goals, Mayawati marches forward with her determined stride, uncaring of the criticism she meets along the way. Confident and extravagant, she has made the colour pink, her 'bobbed' haircut that belongs to a bygone era, blinding solitaires and an array of gun-toting Black Cats her personal trademarks. She has achieved what would have been unthinkable only twenty years ago, and made the Uttar Pradesh landscape a sculptural tribute to B.R. Ambedkar, Kanshi Ram and herself. Ambition and populism are her priorities, and she has worked relentlessly to build her base in national politics. Shikha Trivedy, a features editor at NDTV, has followed Mayawati's political ascendancy for years now. She brings her experience and assessment to this anthology.

Ram Manohar Lohia called Indira Nehru Gandhi a 'goongi gudiya'—how wrong he was! There is a wonderful photograph of Indira Gandhi taken by Raghu Rai, in which Indira Gandhi is seated at her office table with her back to the camera, her khadi-clad congressmen facing her, some sporting Gandhi topis, looking like a bunch of errant, emasculated school boys. This one picture sums up her personality and her time. It is no secret that Indian politicians buckle at the court of strong rulers, women in particular. It also speaks volumes about the supreme strength of the Devi in our society and tradition. The author Sunil Khilnani, who is in the process of writing a historical biography of Jawaharlal Nehru, brings alive some unusual aspects of this icon of the twentieth century.

In a sense, Indira Gandhi's Italian daughter-in-law, Sonia,

grew up in her care. Sonia Gandhi's acute comprehension about the country and people she adopted began at home. She learnt the language, read voraciously, travelled extensively through the Indian hinterland, and today heads the Congress Party. It has been an extraordinary learning process punctuated with personal upheavals and traumas. When unexpectedly widowed, she slid into a private realm of quiet and solitude, and was hardly ever seen in public. Today, Sonia Gandhi is a national leader to reckon with. Circumstances drove her into the fray, and with quiet fortitude and discipline she has risen out of the quagmire of the Indian political scene and carved out a niche for herself. Despite being treated with contempt by her political adversaries, Sonia Gandhi has steadily endeared herself to the people of India by her actions and her dignified persona.

One of the virtues of this civilization is the ability of its people to embrace one and all, as long as they respect what is 'Indian'. Indians trust Sonia Gandhi. Tarun Tejpal, novelist and editor-in-chief of *Tehelka*, traces the political and personal ascendancy of Sonia Gandhi.

This collection of biographical essays is about women who engaged, who created, who continued traditions, who fought for what they believed in, and kept the spirit of India alive. We salute the millions of other women, known and anonymous, who continue to do the same in their own way, and are the pillars of all civilizations.

Malvika Singh

Hai Akhtari!

S. Kalidas

It was probably an All India Radio (AIR) broadcast that sent old Hashmat into a tizzy that night. The unkempt tramp, said to be a love-crazed wastrel from a noble family, was the scourge of Hazratganj-Aminabad. Nobody in Lucknow quite knew where he came from. During the day, when he was more worldly-wise, he sold lemons, onions, garlic and green chillies from house to house. These were special lemons, onions, garlic and chillies, he claimed, in his high-pitched, soulful wail: '*Akhtari ke baag ke nimbu le lo, Akhtari ke baag ke lehsun le lo . . .*' ('Buy lemons from the garden of Akhtari, buy garlic from the garden of Akhtari.')

That night—30 October 1974—on hearing of Akhtari's demise, Hashmat picked up a lump of charcoal and set about writing '*Hai Akhtari!*' in bold calligraphy on the walls of old Lucknow. As he wandered through the chowk in a daze, his voice rang out with the poet Behzad's famous lines: '*Deewana banana hai to deewana bana de, warna kahin qismat tumhe mujh sa na bana de/Ai dekhne walon mujhe hans hans ke na dekho, tumko bhi mohabbat kahin mujh sa na bana de.*' ('If it is madness that you wish for me then make me mad, lest fate make you like me/O onlookers! Do not turn back and stare at me in mirth, lest love also make you mad like me.')

As he meandered through the winding roads and alleys of Lucknow that night, Hashmat wove a comforting cocoon of nostalgia around himself. It was as if he had walked into a twilight world; one that is of the present, yet so deeply embedded in the past. He connected the image of silversmiths pounding *warq* using their wooden mallets with the gracious ritual of welcome with the *paandan* in a courtesan's salon. Had he been sent to one too, in his youth? It was customary for young men of his class to be sent to the *kothas* of *tawaifs* to acquire etiquette, learn the art of polite conversation and appreciate poetry and music from these fascinatingly independent, talented and often very rich and powerful women. Some whispered that Akhtari's father had been a highly respected civil judge.

'*Hamri atariya pe awao sawariya, dekha-dekhi balam hui jaaye*' ('Come to my dwelling, O dark one, and we shall at least exchange glances'), sang Akhtari. As he passed row after row of hanging jasmine and rose gajras, another of Akhtari's lines resonated in his ears: '*Rajaji sowtan ke lambe lambe baal, ulajh mat jaana ho raja ji.*' (O Prince, the rival has long, curly tresses, don't you get entangled, my dear prince.') And much later, in the stillness of the night, as he climbed the rickety staircase of the abandoned haveli where he was a guard of sorts, sharing his space with a goat being fattened for next Id, Hashmat hummed, '*Bahut din beete saiyan ko dekhe . . .*' ('It has been a long time since I set eyes on my beloved . . .')

Twenty years later, virtually to the date, the Government of India was persuaded to release a postage stamp in memory of the great ghazal queen. Her disciple, Rita Ganguli, had organized a significant and memorable event to mark the occasion for which Malka Pukhraj, once the official singer and dancer in Maharaja Hari Singh's court in Kashmir, had come from Lahore, as had an ailing Kaifi Azmi, confined to a wheelchair, from Mumbai. Amidst all the stereotypical platitudes that were mouthed that evening, the bubbling, vivacious spirit of the great Begum was missing. I decided to seek out the many memories of Akhtari Bai Faizabadi, aka Begum Akhtar, by talking to those who knew her intimately through the many different phases of her tempestuous, impassioned, vibrant and stimulating life, complete with all its ups and downs. Here was the story of how this remarkable woman took on challenges, worked the system to subvert patriarchal practices and overcome the many odds that came her way as she pursued the greatest passion of her life, her music.

Faizabad, once the capital of Awadh, near the holy town of Ajudhya, gave us two extraordinary women. One was Umrao Jaan, who descended from Mirza Ruswa's imagination to haunt the pages of history. The other was Begum Akhtar, who became a legend in her lifetime. 'There can be no bai like her ever again,' claimed Jameel Khan Ghaseete, a faqir and devotee of the Begum's from Rampur. 'She might have been a tawaif, but there can never be another like her. Allah be praised! What a voice! She was the Lata [Mangeshkar] of her times,' he insisted. Ghaseete (so named because he had been dragged by his feet—'*ghaseete gaye*'—across a Sufi saint's grave as a child) sang beautifully, and amid the mournful *marsia*s of Meer Anis during Muharram, he would break into Akhtari's saucy love songs with a passion so pure that it could only have been other-worldly.

A few days before she died, Begum Akhtar had been in her suite at Delhi's Marina Hotel. She had left her diary there along with some other personal effects with Saleem Kidwai, the son of a friend from Lucknow who had also become a devoted fan. The first name in the diary was that of Sheila Dhar, a wonderful singer with a resonant timbre in her voice, and the wife of Indira Gandhi's principal secretary, P.N. Dhar. Begum Akhtar was immensely fond of Sheila*ji* (as we all called her) and shared her private anguish, pain and many hidden secrets with her. Sheila*ji*, in her inimitable style, would often regale us with endearing vignettes and tales about the Begum. 'She had such a colourful and lively persona. There was nothing insipid about her. Every emotion came through bold, bright and emphatically, be it love or sorrow. She was never drab, dull, or predictable,' said Sheila*ji*.

'She was a sensitive, cultivated connoisseur of the good things of life,' said Anjali Bannerji, another pupil whose singing perhaps came closest to the Begum's spirit, though Bannerji never sang much professionally. According to Anjali*di*, '*Ammi* [Mummy in Urdu, as those close to her called the Begum] loved good perfumes, good food and drink . . . She hated karela or anything bitter . . . She was very friendly and full of joi de vivre . . . She loved laughing, her laughter was well known. Her pealing laughter was reminiscent of Melina Mercouri.'

We also met the famous light classical singer Shanti Hiranand, the oldest and longest-serving disciple of Begum Akhtar. 'She was the first among thumri and ghazal singers who elevated this genre to the classical arena,' said the sincere and self-effacing Shanti*ji*. Initiated in 1951, he was also the Begum's first formal disciple. Shanti*ji* accompanied us to Lucknow and introduced us to Begum Akhtar's family as well as her lifelong friend, the tabla accompanist Munne Khan. Munne Khan was, for a time, Begum's brother-in-law, having married her sister Shanno. They both found other spouses later.

We met Shanno *apa* in the white colonial house on Havelock Road in Lucknow where Begum Akhtar had lived after her marriage. Shanno *apa* was said to be the Begum's younger sister. She had once, in her youth, been taught some kathak by Achchhan Maharaj, but had never performed at a public venue. Begum Akhtar kept Shanno with her through her life and brought up each one of Shanno's children as she would have her own. Shanno *apa* was a meek, loving girl-Friday to the Begum, managing the kitchen and the household. Said Shanno *apa* about her sister, 'Her personality was such that she loved people . . . But above all, she was a true Allah-wali.'

At the Janpath hotel, where she was staying on a visit to Delhi, Malka Pukhraj lit a cigarette as she reminisced about her friendship with Akhtari. 'She was a very cultured woman and she was never mean. Whenever anyone asked something from her she always graciously obliged. For example, she used to sing this *daadra* [a lilting love song sung in Awadh and eastern UP] that I liked. I said, "Akhtari, please teach me that song," and she immediately taught it to me and wrote down the words . . . *Bahut din beetey saiyan ko dekhe* . . .'

Much time had passed us by since Akhtari's birth in Faizabad in 1914. Her mother, Mushtari Bai, was well trained in both singing and dance. Akhtari was taught under her watchful eye by many masters, prominent among whom were Ata Mohammad Khan of Patiala and Abdul Wahid Khan of the Kirana school. Her youth was spent in Calcutta, where, apart from acting in the theatre she also got some roles in the movies. Greatly inspired by Jaddan Bai, a famous singer of her time and the mother of the actress Nargis, Akhtari was seen in films like *Ek Din Ka Badshah* and *Nal Damayanti* in1933. In quick succession came *Ameena, Mumtaz Begum*

(1934), *Jawaani Ka Nasha* and *Naseeb Ka Chakkar* (1935). But for some reason she dropped a growing film career and moved back home to Lucknow and set up her own salon. By this time she had made a name for herself as a singer, and her 78 rpm records (published under the Megaphone label) were successfully selling across north India. She was being wooed by many princely states to perform and participate in mehfils and mujras. Her dalliance with the film world continued in some manner, and Mehboob Khan cast her along with the dancer Sitara Devi in the film *Roti*, which was released in 1942. Then, almost two decades later, Satyajit Ray persuaded her to play a courtesan in a charming cameo in *Jalsaghar* in 1958.

Munne Khan took us to visit the two-storied house near Cheena Bazaar in Lucknow that Akhtari and her mother had bought for themselves. The ground floor was used as a guest apartment for visiting *ustads*, accompanists and her extended matriarchal family. 'I used to live in a room here when I was married to Shanno,' said Munne Khan. 'Akhtari and her mother, who was addressed as "Bade Saab" [interestingly, a masculine epithet], lived on the first floor. On most evenings, after nine o'clock, Bade Saab would sit chewing paan in the entrance verandah, monitoring access to Akhtari's mehfils. The high point was when the royals came visiting. Once even the Nawab of Rampur, H.H. Raza Ali Khan, was entertained here. The staircase was lined with a red carpet and new furniture was bought for the occasion. Even a new car was bought to fetch him and drop him home. And, when the party ended, Akhtari distributed all the expensive new furniture among the Nawab's entourage and presented the car to his son. In those days she must have showered the nawab with gifts worth 50,000 rupees. You can imagine how the nawab must have reciprocated . . .' Munne Khan recalled.

Akhtari's liaison with Raza Ali Khan of Rampur is well known. 'There was this seven-stringed necklace of Basra pearls in the Rampur collection,' said Sheila*ji*, recalling the story, 'and from the seventh string of the necklace hung a big diamond pendant. The Nawab used to say that if there is anything more lustrous than that diamond, it is the smile of Akhtari.' However, she soon tired of the Nawab and when she left Rampur, 'the necklace left with her'. 'To escape the clutches of the Nawab,' said Munne Khan, 'she turned her gaze towards Abbasi sahib and married him'.

To achieve the goal of becoming Mrs Abbasi was not easy. In this effort, Akhtari was aided by Sayeeda Raza, a well educated aristocratic lady who was then working in the women's section of AIR in Lucknow. Five decades later, when I spoke to her sitting in her elegant South Delhi living room, Sayeeda *apa* (who had later married Meer Mushtaq Ahmed, the Congress mayor of Delhi), recalled Akhtari's wedding to barrister Abbasi. 'One day I was sitting at my desk in AIR when Akhtari entered the room and with great courtesy, asked to speak to me. Just seeing her there thrilled me, for in those days we *pardah-nashin* ladies could never interact freely with professional singing women. Akhtari said she had to speak to me on a private matter, and then politely asked if I knew Ishtiaq Ahmed Abbasi. I said, "Yes, we know him very well and he is quite close to my family." She said, "Good, then please get me married to him." Just like that! Well, I took her request in the direct spirit that it was stated. "I can try," I said, "I can't promise, but I shall certainly try." So I sent for Abbasi sahib and put it to him exactly as Akhtari had put it to me, without any preliminaries. "Ishtiaq *bhai*," I said, "Why don't you marry Akhtari?" As soon as I said that, he picked up my child and started reciting a nursery rhyme: "*Akhto ne pakayi badiyan aur Bakhto ne pakayi daal; Akhto ki badiyan jal gayin, Bakhto ka bura haal*!" [Akhto cooked the *badis* and Bakhto cooked the dal; Akhto's *badis* got burnt, and Bakhto was in a bad way.] He did not answer my question but ate the cake and snacks I had served, and left.'

'Later, I found out,' continued Sayeeda *apa*, 'that they had been meeting secretly for a while and all Akhtari wanted of me was an ally—a strong supporter in society—to further her cause. Of course, there was much gossip. People said I was naive and did not know what I was doing, and suchlike . . . Circumstances changed and rapidly developed, and before we knew it, *shaadi ki naubat ayi* . . . [The play of words here can never be fully conveyed in translation; *naubat* can connote both ill-luck and the auspicious hour. The phrase can read: "the auspicious hour of the wedding arrived" or "the ill-fated wedding took place".] I was present with my husband, as were Akhtari and Ishtiaq bhai; there was the maulvi sahib and one servant, Ghulab. I had put my *shaadi ka dupatta* on her shoulders, and the marriage took place.'

Marriage brought with it the claustrophobic confines of life behind the pardah. Akhtari was now, finally, Begum Akhtar, and music was *haram* (forbidden). 'For a while she found herself playing housewife to the hilt . . . She remained so devoted to and proud of that role right till the end,' recalled an amused Sayeeda *apa*, adding that 'she even started signing her Urdu letters in English as Mrs Ishtiaq Ahmed Abbasi with a flourish!' Did she not miss singing in those years? 'She did miss singing,' said Sayeeda *apa*, 'but more than that she missed the whisky. I panicked, for I had tom-tommed eulogies about her "good conduct" and her chastity. But within the first few years of the marriage she had started drinking and meeting people at her mother's place, and I must say that Ishtiaq *bhai* bore it all stoically . . .'

We then turned to Saleem Kidwai, a historian and close admirer of Begum Akhtar's, to learn about this enigma called Ishtiaq Ahmed Abbasi. Saleem's family had known the Abbasis well and his father, especially, was a close friend of both Ishtiaq Ahmed and Akhtari. 'Abbasi sahib was the talukdar of Kakori,' Saleem told us, adding, 'he was educated in England and had been called to the bar. He wore white bow-ties and rode an old Chevrolet to court. Like all the feudal rich, he too was fond of music and poetry. But I have not heard any reports of his prowess at the bar. Nor do I think his house was ever run on his earnings from his law practice.' According to Sayeeda *apa*, a fervent admirer, 'He was a charming man. He was multifaceted, and could engage with people across the barriers of age and class with grace and ease.'

A few years later, the death of her mother Mushtari sent Akhtari into a fit of deep depression, resulting in bouts of secret drinking. This was followed by the discovery of a tumour in her abdomen that caused her great pain. A doctor prescribed pethidine, a morphine-based drug, to which she got promptly and strongly addicted. Both her sister Shanno and pupil Shanti Hiranand confirmed this on camera to us. 'But, by the Grace of Allah, one day she gave it up herself,' said Shanti, emphasizing her will power.

Slowly, subtle pressure was being mounted on her husband by her admirers that she must be allowed to sing, at least incognito, on the radio. Many officers in the AIR claimed the honour of having brought Akhtari back into the public domain as Begum Akhtar. 'Initially, Abbasi sahib was not convinced this was the right thing to do, but he eventually gave her permission to sing outside of Lucknow,' Sayeeda *apa* said. Did he understand her musical worth? we asked Saleem Kidwai. 'He most certainly did,' said Saleem, 'and he understood it all the more when the world told him so. In fact, he basked in its reflected glory. In a way, he was her ultimate patron.'

So when, after a silence of seven troubled years, Begum Akhtar returned to professional singing on AIR, no one could stop her soaring flight. *'Koyalia tu mat kar pukaar, karejwa laage kataar'* ('O cuckoo, don't you dare call, it pierces my heart like a knife') she sang so eloquently in Awadhi and in Bangla—she had a huge following in Bengal, and sang many popular songs in Bangla. As she grew in stature, Akhtari created small cosmopolitan islands for herself in Delhi, Bombay and Calcutta, where she would be the unquestioned mistress of her fawning audience, away from the disapproving eyes of a staid and strait jacketed Shiite Lucknow. Fans, admirers and hangers-on followed her, and she in turn, would amuse, berate or cajole them depending upon her need, mood or fancy.

Of all the personas she donned, the one she identified with the most was that of the unrequited lover in pain. She was the quintessential *nayika*, the idealized heroine of classical Sanskrit aesthetics. I recall a couplet from Ghalib: *Ishq se tabiyat ne zeest ka maja paya, dard ki dawa payi, dard-e-la-dawa paya.* (Through love, I found the joy of life; I found the panacea for pain, but found that the pain of love was beyond any cure.)

'Love was a condition of life for her,' Sheila Dhar said, adding, 'she could not live without being on the high of love.' More profoundly, Sheila*ji* elaborated, 'It was very important for her to be in love and be pained by it. If love didn't happen, she had to invent it. And if there was no pain, she would invent that too . . . small things may hurt people momentarily, but then, life moves on. She would take the smallest misunderstanding grievously to heart. The slightest injury to her self would torment her like a dagger driven deep into her heart. And this imaginary dagger would remain buried in her till she had extracted every iota of painful pleasure from it.'

'She was very gullible to rumours, and naive in some ways. And she lied all the time, with great abandon, too! "Look, now you are lying again," I would tell her, and she would laugh out gleefully,' recalled Sayeeda *apa*. 'She was extremely giving and affectionate, liberal, large-hearted and a consummate liar—all at once. But when she began to sing, she would make each moment so precious that all her faults were forgotten and forgiven.' Malka Pukhraj, too, endorsed this mesmerizing quality in Akhtari's music that would move her audiences beyond the expected range of emotions. 'When she sang "*Deewana banana hai to deewana bana de*", people literally went mad,' said Pukhraj. Was Hashmat one such victim, I wondered.

'How would one remember Begum Akhtar in the context of her contemporaries, Siddheshwari Devi and Rasoolan Bai?' I asked Sheila*ji*. What were the similarities and what were the contrasts? 'Similarities,' said Sheila*ji*, 'were of the shared repertoire of thumri-daadra, although Siddheshwari*ji* did not sing much ghazal, which was the Begum's forte. What distinguished her was her musical attitude, her stance. It was never overstated. Musicians will agree and Siddheshwari*ji* understood it well herself, that Begum Akhtar could conjure up a grand musical edifice within the borders of a very small canvas. Her music was rendered with graceful ease. It was something that she most effortlessly shared with her audience. Rasoolan was like vintage brandy. Siddheshwari was like a bird of paradise, who threw her soul heavenwards with great energy and passion. Begum Akhtar's technique was much subtler and sophisticated. Her music was stated with great restraint . . .'

Saleem told us about her relations with the great Urdu poets. 'While I did not witness her interaction with Jigar Moradabadi or Shakeel Badayuni, whose ghazals she sang the most, she would tell us about Jigar, especially, with great delight. I did go to meet Firaq Gorakhpuri one day at a hotel in Paharganj where he was staying. She had sung his ghazal the day before at a mehfil and took the recording along for him. She was very close to Kaifi Azmi, there was much jest and flirtation between the two . . . And there were many other poets who became known because she sang their verses.' Was she vain about the fact that she could make or break a poet? 'She was never vain. If she was proud, she never showed it. But yes, if Begum Akhtar sang a poet's verses, what more could he want?' said Saleem.

After the Ghalib centenary celebrations in 1969, for which she released a record of Ghalib's verses, Begum Akhtar became a national icon. Her career was at its peak and she was in great demand for public concerts and private mehfils. But with every public high there were many private lows. She had once again started to sink into fits of depression and heavy drinking. What were her sorrows, we asked Saleem Kidwai. 'I think even she did not know what caused her sorrows,' said Saleem. 'At the end of her life she had achieved pretty much all she wanted. She had her music and her admirers, there was no real want of money. But as in many great artists, she too nursed an undefined "need" that could not be fulfilled. Perhaps, if that need were not there, Begum Akhtar wouldn't have been there either.'

Begum Akhtar died of a heart attack after a concert in Ahmedabad on 30 October 1974. She was buried the next day beside her mother in Lucknow's Pasand Baagh. Her husband, Ishtiaq Ahmed Abbasi, along with many admirers and disciples bade her farewell. '*E Mohabbat tere anjaam pe rona aaya*' ('O Love, your end makes me weep') was her most popular ghazal. With her death ended a reading of love, which she alone had come to epitomize for thousands in India and in Pakistan.

Why Nargis Matters

T.J.S. George

Commercial cinema today puts more emphasis on the commercial, and less on the cinema. Its star component reflects the general culture. For one thing, body building is the dominant element in the net asset value of a male lead, who invariably prefers to go shirtless as often as possible. Stars are available on rent to political parties looking for an opportunistic propaganda boost and a campaign romp or two. From both artistic and sociological perspectives, it is worth pondering why even an Amitabh Bachchan could achieve only success (however stratospheric), not lasting significance. Could it be an inability to see the difference between the two, or a tendency to equate one with the other? Could it be the absence of a purposeful mission, social or aesthetic, without which success becomes essentially vainglorious?

The world was different in the 1950s. Idealism energized talent, and talent inspired idealism. Technology had not become a substitute for ability. There was no special effects department that could make a Terminator out of Arnold Schwarzenegger, no morphological tricks that could convert Kamalahasan into an instant Hydra. An actor had to act. It was part of the folk wisdom of the time that dramatic actors like Dilip Kumar and Balraj Sahni, as well as 'character artistes' like Lalita Pawar and Achla Sachdev, would spend hours studying their parts and perfecting the nuances of their performances.

Not surprisingly, a thousand flowers bloomed in the years that immediately followed Independence. Directors like Bimal Roy and K.A. Abbas pioneered the romantic-neorealist genre of cinema, directly influenced by the European masters in general, and Vittorio De Sica in particular. Composers like Naushad endowed their music with classical dimensions. Lyricists like Sahir Ludhianwi and Shakeel Badayuni were not just film lyricists, but poets of considerable worth. The erratic Kishore Kumar's simultaneous brilliance in different departments was something of a marvel. For that matter, where has there been a comedian who could rival the versatility and finesse of Johny Walker?

If this sounds like a throwback to the old-is-gold cliche, so be it. The 1950s were indeed a golden age, described as such and compared to the golden age of the 1930s, when New Theatres, Bombay Talkies and Prabhat lit up the skies and filled them with stars of the calibre of Devika Rani and K.L. Saigal. Those decades attained a measure of significance because cinema recognized its social responsibility. Pictures like Shantaram's *Amrita Manthan* (1934), Bombay Talkies' *Acchut Kanya* (1936) and Mehboob Khan's *Ek Hi Rasta* (1939) found worthy successors in the second golden age with Zia Sarhadi's *Humlog* (1951), Bimal Roy's *Do Bigha Zamin* (1953) and Mehboob's *Mother India* (1957). A good deal of trash came out of those years, but the thinkers made up for the titillators.

The stars kept pace—on the female side as well as the male. It took a dedicated producer-director-bureaucrat named Mohan Bhavnani to help break the social taboo that kept 'respectable women' out of cinema. In *Vasant Sena,* which he produced in 1931, he scored a triumph for which he is yet to be fully recognized; he persuaded the socially prominent Kamaladevi Chattopadhyay and Enakshi Rama Rau to appear before the camera. But that was not enough for him. He wanted an educated lady to take to films as a profession and thereby set an example. This he achieved when Durga Khote, the Cathedral School-educated wife of the upper-crust lawyer Viswas Khote, agreed to star in Bhavnani's *Trapped* (1931).

That debut led to the opening of the floodgates. Devika Rani, who had teamed up with Himanshu Rai two years earlier in Germany, became the queen of the first golden age not only because of her histrionic capabilities, but also her aristocratic pedigree. She was the daughter of Col. M.N. Chowdury, surgeon-general, who had sent her off to England at the age of nine in order to bring her up as a proper English lady. Trained at the Royal Academy of Dramatic Arts and later in Germany, she was as educated as anyone could be. She was now joined by a galaxy of stars—Shanta Apte, Leela Chitnis, Shobhana Samarth, Kannanbala, Sadhana Bose. The 1950s saw a line-up just as glittering—Meena Kumari, Madhubala, Kamini Kaushal, Geeta Bali, Waheeda Rahman, Nutan.

And Nargis. How did this progeny of the kothewali class of professional singers transcend her custom-ordained destiny, rise above her extraordinarily gifted fellow artistes, rise even above the aristocratic Devika Rani, and become the first lady of the second golden age? K.A. Abbas had noted that she was not a great actress to start with. Yet she became not only 'the greatest star of our film industry', as Balraj Sahni described her, but also an icon of her times, with an assured place among the great women of India.

Genes certainly had something to do with it—genes, and

a natural ambition for excellence that grew from them. Her mother, Jaddan Bai, imperious and colourful, sensed early on that life ought to be about more than singing and dancing for the entertainment of northern India's zamindars. She became so proficient in singing, especially thumri, that when she was on a visit to Calcutta, K.L. Saigal listened to her and told friends about the classical character of her music.

Another Punjabi who attended that soiree was smitten by the singer as well as the song. Uttamchand Mohanchand (Mohan Babu) from Rawalpindi was on his way to England to study medicine. He cancelled all his plans and persuaded Jaddan Bai, already a mother of two boys, to marry him. Their daughter Nargis inherited a capacity to both love profoundly and develop a sensitive attachment to books and education. These traits, combined with an ability to dream, which she imbibed from her mother, formed the foundations of Nargis's personality.

It was of course the aesthetic side of that personality that made her a star. But there were other aspects of her life that made her unlike any other star. She made contributions of her own as a woman, as a mother and wife, as a citizen and as a committed social worker. Her multiple involvements gave her a sense of direction which several of her talented contemporaries missed. Waheeda Rahman was one of the few who found fulfilment in her career and went into graceful retirement. Madhubala and Nutan were overtaken by illnesses, while Meena Kumari fell prey to excesses with the bottle. Nargis always had worthy causes to pursue. That was why, even though cancer brought her life to a painful end, she filled the fifty-two years of her life with accomplishments of a lasting kind.

First and foremost, she was an artiste. Her appearance in

her mother's production *Talashe Haq* in 1935 at the age of six may be considered no more than a matter of record. (Her name appeared in the credits as Baby Rani. Among family and close friends she was always known by the pet name 'Baby'.) At fourteen, she was dreaming of joining college and becoming a doctor. It took a full day for Mehboob Khan to persuade her to accept the heroine's role in his film *Taqdeer* (1943). Mehboob also gave her a new screen name. She obviously could not be featured as Baby Rani. Nor was her official name, Fatima Abdul Rashid, attractive enough for cinema. Her father had named her Tejeswari Mohan. That too was considered unsuitable. Mehboob finally chose a one-word name: Nargis. Half a dozen indifferent films followed. Then came milestones in the history of Hindi cinema, beginning with *Aag* in 1948, and *Andaz* and *Barsaat* in 1949. The magic had begun.

Any consideration of Nargis's film career should take two of its essential ingredients into account—the temper of India in the 1950s, and the creativity of her association with Raj Kapoor. The euphoria of a newly independent country had a salutary impact on cinema. As a dramatic art that blends myriad skills into a single compendium of experience, cinema needs a confluence of talents and a commitment of the talented.

The artists, technicians and visionaries who converged in cinema in the years immediately following Independence could not have asked for a more propitious moment in terms of opportunities. Despite some Gandhian leaders who saw cinema as sinful, optimism was the prevailing mood, and everyone was a reformist. Liberal themes, imaginative treatment and creative virtuosity could expect instant acceptance. There was a great coming together of mood and man. There was an all-round striving towards fresh goals, an urge to venture into new areas. Cinema became inspirational.

It was in such an atmosphere that destiny brought Nargis and Raj Kapoor together. No hero-heroine team has given more electric moments to Indian cinema than this pair. There were other pairings like Dev Anand and Suraiya; Dilip Kumar and Kamini Kaushal. But Nargis and Raj Kapoor complemented each other, brought out the best in each other as no other star team did. Nargis told an interviewer in 1954: 'Before I started work with Raj, my ideas were bottled up. There was no one with whom I could discuss them freely. With Raj it is different. We seem to have practically the same views and ideas, the same outlook on all subjects.'

Raj Kapoor for his part was too conscious of his prerogatives as a man to concede much to a woman. But there can be no doubt that Nargis was the finest artistic asset he had under his R.K. Films banner. This became clear after the two broke up around 1957. Nargis went on to make *Mother India* that year, considered by many to be the zenith of her career. In contrast, not a single film of note came out of R.K. Studios after Nargis left. Indeed, *Ab Dilli Dur Nahi*, which came out in the year of the break-up, is generally considered the poorest of R.K. Films's offerings. *Jis Desh Mein Ganga Behti Hai* (1960) had the usual formula ingredients, but was without the easy spontaneity that made his earlier movies so heart-warming. This film pointed to a fundamental shift in Raj Kapoor's very approach to cinema. He now found resorting to tawdry sex appeal necessary. Padmini's 'assets' were used with a blatancy never seen during the Nargis phase.

Clearly, the Nargis-Raj Kapoor combination was good for cinema, just as their break-up was bad for Raj Kapoor's cinema. While it lasted, it was the most celebrated love affair of the time. So perfect was the chemistry between them that even ordinary poses struck instinctively by them became classic images of India's entertainment lore. One of these poses became the famous logo of R.K. Films: Nargis flowing over the arm of a violin-bearing Raj. Another, a simple shot from *Shree 420*, showing the two of them sheltering under an umbrella in heavy rain, tugs at heartstrings for completely inexplicable reasons.

What is undeniable is that Nargis and Raj Kapoor brought an unprecedented openness to screen romance. Meena Kumari, the prototype of the romantic heroine, was forever sacrificing and suffering. She was aptly described as the 'tragedy queen' because with her romance was inseparable from tragedy.

Nargis and Raj Kapoor revolutionized the concept of romance by boldly projecting love as a prerogative of the young. They looked as though they were made for the part. She was vulnerably feminine if also happily submissive. He was impishly masculine if also happily submissive. Adoring each other unabashedly, they turned romance into a joyous celebration. Instead of feeling guilty, they revelled in it. They did retain the concept of pain as part of the ecstasy of love; it would not be Indian otherwise. But the Nargis heroine was proud of her emotions, full of self-esteem and ready to fight for her right to love and be loved.

In *Barsaat*, an entirely new idiom of screen romance was at work. His fingers tenderly probing around her mouth, her head tilting in a gesture of total submission, his hands fondly rustling her hair, her eyes catching fire as she looked at him— this was intuitive romancing, honest and unpremeditated. In the sixteen pictures in which they starred together, love was not always the central theme. Yet the wondrous aura surrounding the pair gave the films an extraordinary pitch and panache.

Raj Kapoor's place in Indian cinema is historical, entrenched and unique. It may therefore seem invidious to suggest that his artistic wellsprings were not as deep as Nargis's. Yet that conclusion is inevitable when their contrasting trajectories after the break-up are taken into consideration. *Mother India* is proof of Nargis's unmatched ability to summon up inner reserves of inspiration and propel herself to new levels of excellence, Raj Kapoor or no Raj Kapoor. Her role covered the entire span of life, from a young wife to an old woman. It called for a complete range of emotions, from romance and rustic toughness to a manifestation of womanly resolve that would prompt her to shoot her own son when he tried to abduct a girl. She brought a raw power to bear on her performance. It was a Nargis who had attained a fullness of artistic maturity.

That Nargis scaled the summit of achievement with her performance in *Mother India* was acknowledged by all. Abroad, she won an award at the Karlovy Vary festival. At home, Dilip Kumar said, 'Her best picture is *Mother India*. Her second best picture is *Mother India*. Her third best picture is *Mother India*.' Thirty years after the picture was released, a reviewer wrote, '*Mother India* is to Nargis what *The Godfather* is to Marlon Brando and *The Sound of Music* to Julie Andrews. The role and the film are inextricably entwined in the mind of the public so much so that the two are almost one.'

When *Mother India* was made, Nargis was two years short of thirty. The woman in her had been yearning for fulfilment of a different kind, and it was not forthcoming from Raj Kapoor. She knew he was married and had children of his own, yet she hoped to marry him and raise a family. She never looked upon her relationship with him as an affair, because she was always serious about it. Her intentions were honourable. She wanted to raise a family the right and proper way. Arrangements of convenience such as the Hema Malinis of a later generation would accept were not good enough for her. She had to go about it without compromising her dignity as a woman. But by 1956 it was clear that nothing of the sort was possible with Raj Kapoor. When his attention was openly diverted to 'variety from the south', she decided to end the relationship.

Initially, the parting must have wrenched her emotionally. But the challenge of *Mother India* gave her something to concentrate on. Her own strength of character shored her up. Work and personal resoluteness helped her emerge rapidly as a complete woman. She went through a renewal. On the sets of *Mother India* she met Sunil Dutt. His genuineness and simplicity made an impression on her. Her compassion for his sick sister moved him. In early 1958 they got married according to Arya Samaj rites.

From Nargis's point of view, the importance of that union cannot be overstated. There was nothing in life she wanted more than marriage and children. As a teenager she was a tomboy, but she used to spend every spare moment with the children of her two brothers in their Marine Drive flat. When she began acting in the early films, she took charge of the children, financing and supervizing their education, choosing their clothes and toys, organizing their outings. Her sense of family was as strong as her maternal instincts. With Sunil Dutt now her husband, she could at last realize her lifelong ambition. As her friend and co-star K.N. Singh put it, 'With marriage, it was like she had reached home. She thought God had come to earth in the form of Sunil Dutt. So much did she worship him.' Nargis, the heart-throb of a generation, would glow with excitement if someone called her 'Mrs Dutt'.

She did make a film or two after marriage, but this was to help her brothers. These exceptions apart, her retirement from the film industry was real. Sunil Dutt would not have it any other way, for he was conventional enough to insist that, as the husband, it was his duty to be the family's provider. Nargis's own resolve to remain a wife and mother was beautifully underlined by her when the great S.S. Vasan of Gemini Studios in Madras approached her with a film offer. Vasan was a sort of 'king emperor' of cinema. He never approached a star directly. He flew to Bombay to make an exception for Nargis, hoping that the gesture alone would clinch the matter. He gave her a blank cheque as well. Nargis teased him for a while and then said, 'Vasan Saab, I am completely tied up with three films right now. They are called Sanju, Anju and Priya. I just cannot do another film now.' Vasan was speechless.

The award of a Padma Shri to her in 1958 kindled a latent desire in husband and wife to play an active role in public life. In separate and different ways, both had already come under the influence of Jawaharlal Nehru and Indira Gandhi. Sunil Dutt was inspired by what he perceived as idealism in Nehru. Nargis became close to Indira so much so that she and her husband remained steadfast supporters of the Emergency and of Indira when she was out in the wilderness after the electoral defeat that followed it. In time Nargis would become a nominated member of the Rajya Sabha and Sunil Dutt an elected member of the Lok Sabha. But essentially, both were political innocents, motivated only by their friendship with Indira on the one hand and their desire to be of some service to the country on the other.

Eventually, it was not in politics but in their work for the handicapped that they found their forte. There was a strong instinct in Nargis to acquire medical qualifications. Perhaps it was a continuation of her father's aborted ambition to become a doctor. Even after marriage, Sunil Dutt recalled, she had expressed a desire to go abroad and become a qualified nurse so that she could attend to the sick and needy.

She soon found herself involved in social work focused on underprivileged children and the handicapped. She discovered that it was an interest that absorbed her husband as well. Together they set up a school for poor children in a plot of land which they bought in Bandra. They also set up the Centre for Special Education for Spastics. When the Spastics Society of India was established in Bombay, she was nominated as one of the promoters. Neither she nor Sunil Dutt treated this work as mere social feathers in their caps. They were seriously committed to it. Nargis conducted herself as a nurse when she was involved in the care of spastic children. She was, in the opinion of colleagues, 'professional' in her approach. Never missing a committee meeting, she always studied the files, understood the details and was ready with ideas on how to expand and improve the Spastics Society's work.

She also immersed herself in the activities of the Bharat Scouts and Guides, the War Widows' Association and the Meena Kumari Memorial for the Blind. This kind of social service was rare then, and is perhaps even rarer today. Among the busiest stars of the time, Nargis and Sunil Dutt found time to work for the less privileged, often spending their own money to see the programmes through. It was an approach to life that contrasted with the approach of today's stars, be they of film or cricket, who make more money but have less interest in the suffering of their fellow human beings.

For Nargis, life was incomplete without her social work.

The way she threw herself into it was indicative of the transformation of her persona after marriage. Only now did she seem to have come into her own. It was a new Nargis, a complete Nargis, happy and satisfied in a way she never was when she was at the pinnacle of filmic glamour. The film star had metamorphosed into an independent woman with clear-cut views about life, people and priorities. Nargis had found herself.

But this sense of fulfilment was destined to be short-lived. Tragedy struck in 1979 when Nargis was diagnosed as having, first, obstructive jaundice and then, cancer of the pancreas. The best treatment in New York brought only temporary relief. Nargis was in prolonged pain, necessitating sedation. Her plight turned pitiable with her beloved son, Sanjay Dutt, sinking into the half-life of hallucinogens. In time he would bounce back and become a health freak and a macho screen hero. But Nargis was denied the pleasure of witnessing her son's triumph. All she had in her last days was the feeling that the idyll of her family life was crumbling around her even as she lay fighting for her life. It was a fight she could not win. She slipped into the silence of her final sleep on 3 May 1981.

Arundhati Roy has said that thirty-one is a viable die-able age. Maybe it is. But fifty-two certainly was not a die-able age. Not when the life that death snatched belonged to someone like Nargis, who was still brimming with promise and plans. When it did happen, it seemed to highlight not so much the majesty of human suffering as its pointlessness. But in a poignant kind of way, even the shadow of death brought out the uniqueness of Nargis's mind.

After weeks of despair in a cancer ward in New York, with kidney and heart complications adding to the hopelessness of the situation, five surgical operations shattering her mentally as well as physically, the Dutts could only think of going home, where she could at least die in the bosom of her family. When the doctors allowed them to travel, they spent a few days preparing for the long flight home. On one of their outings she surprised her husband with the remark, 'You never did the right thing in bringing me here.' Pressed to explain, she said, 'There must be millions of sufferers in our country who must be as important to their families as I am to you. But they don't get medical facilities like I got . . . If I live, I must take this up with the government and with Madam Gandhi. Such facilities must become available in India.'

The human qualities that added value to Nargis's work as a film personality were emphasized by all the public figures, film industry leaders and editorial writers who assessed her career after her passing. No star of her time—indeed, no star of any time—devoted time and attention to public and social causes in the way Nargis did. Compassion came naturally to her. At one level she was famous for getting oversized food containers from home, so that the light boys and stage hands on the set could get a hearty meal during their lunch breaks. At another level, news that a colleague's wife or child was sick would see Nargis taking charge of the patient until recovery was assured. If a child was handicapped in any way, she would drop everything and make arrangements for the child's care and treatment. This was a humanist who happened to become a star.

The connections and resources Nargis garnered as a star were used for her humanitarian programmes, and this was the key to her success as a social worker. This was also partly responsible for the importance she achieved in the context of her time. But of course, the main plank of that importance was her contribution as an artiste. She embodied the period in which Indian cinema grew out of its 'staginess' and took its place on the world scene. The romantic-neorealist genre of cinema reached its apotheosis through the authenticity imparted to its portrayal by stars like Nargis.

Substance in cinema is considered to be the natural domain of directors, not actors. Yet, stars who give wing to new concepts in their metier exert influence not inferior to that of directors. It would be difficult, for example, to look upon Marlon Brando as just another actor who did well in his time. This is more so in Indian cinema, because stars often participate in conceptualization and story development. Nargis's contribution to the making of R.K. Films's classics was by no means inconsequential. The achievements of Raj Kapoor were, without exception, the achievements of the Raj-Nargis team. Without her, the R.K. banner simply lost its wind.

The significance of stars who go beyond their immediate career demands and become part of a larger artistic current, be they Greta Garbo or Humphrey Bogart, Devika Rani or Nargis, needs to be examined in a context that transcends the exigencies of popular taste and the particular years of their action. Nargis's effectiveness as an artiste was related to, and enhanced by, her integrity as an individual. By embracing a wider domain than her contemporaries did, she became larger than the sum of her parts. The best actors embody the characteristics of their own cultures. Nargis epitomized the Indian woman in her strength and weakness, her aspirations and her inherent dignity. Inasmuch as these are deathless values, her representative status is unrestricted by time. She lives.

A Life in Service

Subhashini Ali Sahgal

My mother's father, S. Swaminadhan, was a Palghat Iyer. His father, a lower-rung employee in the district court of Palghat, passed away when his son was only a young boy. My mother's great-grandfather, P. Govinda Menon, recognized his exceptional intelligence and helped him, both financially and with words of encouragement, to complete his studies. He subsequently won scholarships to study Law in Edinburgh and was awarded a doctorate from Harvard.

When he returned to Madras, his fellow-caste men insisted that he perform the ritual *prayishchit* for having sinned by crossing the oceans to go abroad where, no doubt, he had been exposed to every kind of pollution. Not only did he refuse to do any such thing, but openly declared that even if he did agree, he would attend the ceremony with a beefsteak in one hand and a bottle of whisky in the other! He made this threat despite being a lifelong vegetarian and teetotaller, but of his own choice.

Grandfather soon became a successful lawyer in Madras, and his thoughts often turned to P. Govinda Menon, his benefactor in Kerala. He was keen to repay him in some way for the kindness and generosity that he had shown him, and decided to visit him. If he had an unmarried daughter, he would offer himself as a prospective son-in-law.

By the time my grandfather arrived at Vadakath House in Anakara village in Palghat district, my great-grandfather had been dead for several years. My great-grandmother, however, was very much alive. She was A.V. Lakshmikutty Amma, the beautiful, capable and strong-willed mistress of Vadakath House, which she had shared with her late husband in the matrilineal tradition of the Malabar Nairs. My grandfather had often met her as a young boy, and she had left a strong impression on his adolescent mind. In fact, it may have been this impression even more than his sense of gratitude to her husband that made him so keen to marry one of her daughters.

My great-grandmother was delighted to see him. He had been a favourite of hers, and she was happy to hear of his success. He was made welcome in the house and after he had offered his condolences and asked after the welfare of the other members of the family, he came to the point of his visit. My great-grandmother was quite surprised by his offer. She told him that unfortunately all her daughters, except for the youngest, were married. The youngest, Ammu, was just a little girl.

My grandfather asked if he could meet her anyway. Ammu turned out to be a self-confident fourteen-year-old. My grandfather teasingly asked her if she would marry him. To his surprise, and to the consternation of everyone else around her, she said she would—but only if he promised to fulfil her conditions. Playing along, he asked her what her conditions were. She replied confidently: I will not live in a village ever again but in a big city like Madras; I will be taught English by an Englishwoman; and, I will be free to do as I please. From what little I know about my grandfather, her cheeky reply and her conditions must have delighted him.

He accepted every one of them, and this was how my grandmother promised to marry him.

Once this was settled, my grandfather had many things to attend to. A marriage between a Brahmin man and a Nair woman was unthinkable. At the time a 'sambandham' between the two was an accepted social convention. According to this tradition, younger sons from Brahmin families were not allowed to marry Brahmin girls, but entered into relationships with Nair women. The woman would continue to stay in her ancestral home and bear his children. Looking after the children was entirely the mother's responsibility, and they would grow up to inherit their respective shares in her share of the ancestral property. Not only did they have nothing to do with their Brahmin relatives, but their own father never deigned to touch them as this would 'pollute' him!

Nothing could have been more abhorrent to my grandfather than the repugnant caste system and the many inequalities that it engendered. He was determined to ensure that his own marriage to Ammu was legal in every sense of the word, and that she and their children became his legal heirs. He therefore embarked on a long and tortuous course that brought him to the brink of a nervous breakdown.

The feudal lord of the Nairs of the area was the Zamorin of Calicut, and it is to him that my grandfather took his request. Not surprisingly, a hornet's nest of controversy, viciousness and furious debate was stirred up in the Madras Presidency, of which Malabar was at that time a part. Eventually, the Zamorin gave his grudging consent, but the Brahmin community boycotted the wedding and the feast that followed. But the marriage took place, and my grandparents left for Madras soon after. My grandfather, however, was still not satisfied that all had been done to make his marriage legally secure and so, at the first opportunity, he took Ammu to England and married her all over again in a registry office.

In a few years their son, Govind, and daughter, Lakshmi, were born. They were followed by another daughter and son, Mrinalini and Subram. All four children were brought up absolutely equal, with no gender biases whatsoever. The only difference was that the two boys were sent off to England very young, first to school and then to university. While Govind stoically held back his tears when he was sent off, Subram wept throughout the long boat journey. The girls were spared these tragic separations and went to the best school that Madras had to offer.

Lakshmi was a beautiful young girl who turned into an even more beautiful woman. She had long hair, large eyes that retained their innocence and purity even when she had aged, and a glowing complexion. And she had very fair skin. The combination of all these factors ensured that she was drowned in compliments, 'oohs' and 'aahs' practically from the moment she was born. It would have been understandable if she had turned into an insufferable, spoilt brat, but incredibly, this did not happen.

Her brother Govind, a man more given to acerbic wit than pretty compliments, said about her with a sense of wonder quite foreign to him, 'She is the only beautiful woman I know who doesn't have a vain bone in her body. Vanity is something completely foreign to her. She has always been totally unspoilt.' She was one of those people who simply did what came most naturally to her—living for others—without being in the least bit concerned with either recompense or recognition.

Meanwhile, her mother, Ammu, had become one of the leading lights of Madras society. She was the first woman to get a driving licence and own a car. She had a smart coach drawn by two well-matched horses which she drove herself along Marina beach. She played tennis and threw successful parties at which the elite, both British and Indian, played dumb charades and had a 'jolly good time'. But by no means was she an empty-headed social butterfly. An intelligent woman who always maintained a link with her roots, her village, her large family, the different members of which belonged to various economic and social classes, and who was free of all forms of snobbery, she was soon attracted to the Swadeshi movement in Madras. It was the social content of the movement that attracted her as much as the political. Issues of caste and gender oppression struck an immediate chord, and the agitations against foreign liquor and cloth won her wholehearted support. Lakshmi vividly remembers a huge bonfire in their front lawn, stoked by an unending stream of lacy frocks, pretty dolls and chiffon saris. She remembers feeling both miserable and elated, and reminisces that when it was all over she did not feel any regret.

This bonfire is one of Lakshmi's early memories, but there are others as well. Because their school was close to her father's brother's house, Lakshmi and her sister, Mrinalini, would go there in the afternoon to eat lunch, which was sent from home. One day, she asked her mother if they could eat sitting on the floor at their own home as they did at their uncle's. It was then that her mother realized that her Brahmin in-laws were making her half-caste children sit on the floor. She was furious, and complained to her husband. He told her that the best way to teach them a lesson was to make sure that the children's tiffin always contained plenty of meat and lots of bones!

But, of course, caste prejudice, while it may have emanated from the Brahmins, did not end with them. Lakshmi remembers her grandmother (who taught her to swim in the natural pond at Vadakath) telling her not to touch scheduled caste children because if she did she would go blind. Of course, Lakshmi immediately ran out of the house and, hugging a little child returned shouting, 'See, I'm not blind!'

Dr Swaminadhan died in 1930, when Ammu was only thirty years old. His death revealed many unusual attributes to his personality, as had his life. Before his death he told his wife that on no account was she to break her bangles, shave her head, stop applying *kum kum* on her forehead or stop wearing coloured saris. He also promised her that she would never need to ask either of her sons, or anyone else, for any kind of financial help as long as she lived. She would also never have to be dependent on others to provide a roof over her head.

As a result, Ammu was an independent woman who lived in her own home till her death many years later. Dr Swaminadhan proved to be an exemplary father and grandfather. He left his moveable wealth equally divided between his daughters and sons, and his property equally divided between their children. In the year 1930 what he did was truly unheard of.

When Lakshmi finished studying science in college in 1932, she had the option of going abroad for her further studies (as had been promised by her father), but she was determined to become a doctor. She joined medical college the same year. Her college years were eventful. Apart from the pressure of studies, political activity surrounded her both at home and outside. By this time her mother had become active in the Congress Party and in the All India Women's

Conference. But Lakshmi was attracted to a more militant brand of politics. She had heard and was impressed by Subhash Chandra Bose, the charismatic Congress president.

Closer to home, Sarojini Naidu's sister, Suhasini Chattopadhyay, the first woman to join the Communist Party of India, spent some of her underground years as Ammu's guest in Madras. She spent hours talking to Lakshmi, who was enthralled by her tales of the Russian Revolution and the heroic martyrdom of the German Communists. She regaled her with renditions not only of the 'Internationale' (in her impressive baritone), but also 'Somebody over there really loves me', which she sang to the 'wretched' policemen who stood outside the house waiting to nab her as she came out!

Communist ideas and ideals could not but appeal to Lakshmi, who was often caught stealing food and clothes from the house to distribute to poor patients in the government hospital where she was now an intern. (A sad postscript to this: when Ammu was old and very ill, lapsing in and out of a coma, Lakshmi was in Madras looking after her. One night the nurse removed her gold chain and ring which she thought were chafing her skin, and gave them to Lakshmi for safekeeping. Ammu recovered during the night, and her fingers started searching for the chain and the ring. The nurse told her reassuringly, 'I have given them to your daughter.' This made Ammu wake up with a start and she said, 'Take them back quickly, otherwise she will give them to the Communists!')

Meanwhile, Lakshmi's turbulent private life was pushing her in different directions. In her fourth year of medical college, she met a dashing Tata Air pilot who fell head over heels in love with her and, without much thought, she married him. When I asked her why on earth she had done such a thing she said, 'Well, it was actually just a pleasant flirtation between us, but my mother was so upset and critical that I thought it would be better to marry him. So I did.' Later on I came to know that the pilot would often fly over her home, showering it with rose petals! This must have added considerably to his other attractions. Unfortunately, however, she spent barely three months of married life in Bombay and then returned to her medical studies in Madras. Soon she became romantically involved with a fellow student a year senior to her. However, because her pilot-husband was not agreeable to a divorce, they could not marry. This drove them to an attempted suicide which they fortunately survived, following which he went off to Singapore to practise medicine.

Lakshmi's favourite cousin, Kutty, and his much-loved wife, Padmini, were also in Singapore. She took advantage of this to leave Madras and follow her friend there. Soon they had established a successful practice and a happy life together. Lakshmi had a large number of poor patients, migrant Indians who worked in the plantations or in various menial and ill-paid jobs. She was also closely associated with the India Independence League, which functioned as a branch of the Congress Party in Singapore.

Those were momentous times. The war was raging on the Eastern Front, and the Japanese seemed to be growing stronger with each passing day. Singapore, however, was believed to be an invincible British bastion. In the autumn of 1942, however, this illusion lay shattered when the Japanese bombed the airport and many of the British planes parked there, forcing the British army to surrender after a series of lightning attacks. The bulk of this army and many of its officers were actually Indians. While they had fought bravely and loyally for 'their King', they could not help but be influenced by the patriotic winds that were blowing throughout the length and breadth of India. Many of the officers were only too conscious of the racism of the British officers, and had often suffered humiliation at their hands.

After the surrender by the British, the Japanese made the Indian men and officers a breathtaking offer. They were prepared to help them constitute an army for the liberation of India. Furious debates raged throughout the POW camp. Many of the officers came from families that had served the British for generations. They suffered bitter divisions of loyalty. Many of them could not bear the thought of being viewed as traitors. Others felt that their primary loyalty was to their emerging nation; that enslaved peoples had the inherent right to revolt.

My father, Prem Sahgal, was one of the young officers who took the lead in convincing the others that they should opt for an army of liberation. In his student days in Lahore, he had been a courier for the young revolutionaries around Bhagat Singh. Later on, disillusioned by Gandhi's tactics which he considered cowardly, he resumed his studies and joined the army. For some reason he felt that this was the only place where he could conclusively prove that he was as good as—if not better than—his 'White masters'.

As part of the group of officers that accepted the Japanese offer, my father was granted a certain amount of freedom and could meet other Indians in Singapore. One of them was Lakshmi, who immediately became involved in all the discussion and debate surrounding the birth of the Indian National Army (INA). She agreed passionately with my father and, along with other members of the India Independence League, assisted him and his colleagues in every way possible.

There were several difficulties, though. The senior-most

officer to have accepted the Japanese offer, General Mohan Singh, had second thoughts and opted out. The Japanese inducted an old Indian revolutionary, Rash Behari Bose, who had escaped capture at the hands of the British by going into self-exile in Japan, and brought him to Singapore to head the INA. But he had been out of touch with India for too long. He realized that he was not acceptable to the officers and men of the INA. To his eternal credit he suggested to the Japanese that they somehow bring Subhash Chandra Bose from Berlin to Singapore.

While under house arrest after the call for the Quit India Movement was given in August 1942, Subhash Chandra Bose dramatically escaped to Europe through Afghanistan and Central Asia. On arrival in Berlin, he organized the Indian students in Germany to form the INA. Working on the theory that 'my enemy's enemy is my friend', he attempted to persuade the German government and Hitler to support this army's entry into India. Logistics and the war situation just did not allow this to happen, and when the Japanese request to send Bose to Singapore came, the German government was only too happy to accede to it. He left by submarine at a time when the war at sea was raging, accompanied by his German interpreter and secretary, a young Hyderabadi called Abid Husain, who confessed once their submarine was duly submerged that not only could he not swim but that he had an innate terror of water. To this Bose replied that they would probably not have much swimming to do if their submarine was torpedoed. Bose and Abid finally arrived in Tokyo, from where they left for Singapore, arriving there on 3 July 1943.

On 6 July, the India Independence League in Singapore organized a huge rally. All the men and officers who had rallied on the side of the INA were there in military formation, and so was almost every member of the Indian community in the city. Netaji, as Bose was now known, made an inspiring speech in which he promised them their freedom in exchange for blood. He also appealed to the Indian community to contribute generously so that the INA could be truly Indian, and not just an army of Japanese stooges.

That evening, Netaji met with the leaders of the India Independence League and placed his astonishing proposal before them. He was determined to create and train a regiment of Indian women. The Japanese had laughed him out of court but he remained firm, determined that he would ask his own countrymen to contribute to the cost of this unusual regiment. He asked the League's members to suggest the name of a woman who could lead the regiment—for the moment, this was the only problem he could foresee. He was convinced that once a leader was identified, recruitment would not be a problem. Lakshmi's name was suggested. The sense of elation created by the enthusiastic response to Netaji's inspiring call for sacrifice completely enthralled Lakshmi, and she met him the very next day. Even before he had completed his proposal, she accepted. All thoughts of her medical practice and of the life she shared with her friend were completely overwhelmed by the conviction that this was somehow the moment that her entire life had been leading up to. She continued at home for a few months, but all her waking hours were spent in the INA office. One can only imagine what her partner went through.

Many years later, he came to Delhi. He was very ill and confined to his son's house, allowed only a short drive in the evenings. My uncle Kutty was also in Delhi at the time, and the two friends would occasionally meet. The doctor from Singapore mentioned to Kutty that he would like to meet

Lakshmi before he died. A few weeks later, Lakshmi was in town and the three of them met over tea at Kutty's house. The tea lasted a long time, and his son (with whom he was staying) became extremely worried when his father did not return at the usual time. He told me later that when his father did come home, he looked radiant. All he said with a smile to his son was, 'I met Lakshmi.'

Lakshmi was appointed the commanding officer of what became the Rani of Jhansi Regiment, and later joined Netaji's Council of Ministers of the Provisional Government of Azad Hind as its only woman minister. Her friendship with Prem Sahgal also matured but, according to her, there was little time for romance.

The recruitment of the Ranis for the women's regiment is an inspiring illustration of what the most ordinary women can do when given even the slightest opportunity. When the news spread in Singapore that such a regiment was to be formed, hundreds of young women from the city-state and from different parts of Malaya offered themselves for training and battle. They belonged to a range of social classes and communities but were, for the most part, poor or lower middle class South Indian women. (Even my aunt Padmini, a mother of two young girls, an asthmatic and the most peaceable of women, insisted on receiving arms training!) The response was so overwhelming that many of them had to be turned away, weeping. Training started with an initial batch of 300 women in Singapore. A few months later, another 100 were recruited in Rangoon, Burma and a training camp was started there. Finally, there were more than 1200 recruits. Of them 200 were trained as nurses, though all of them received military training as demanding as what was expected of the male soldiers. The Rani of Jhansi Regiment was not a 'nursing' unit, as many people believe. It was trained for combat and sent to fight on the Burma front.

Manavati Arya was born and brought up in Burma. She was a member of the India Independence League, and later joined the INA in an administrative capacity. She too had received some military training and had led a section of women soldiers to the front. She often met Lakshmi during her visits to Rangoon and other parts of Burma, and has many memories of her. She laughs and says that Lakshmi struggled heroically to learn Hindi, but could never achieve fluency. (A problem that persists till today, despite having lived in Uttar Pradesh for the past fifty years or more!) She remembers that when Lakshmi arrived in Rangoon after the headquarters shifted there, two big suitcases of her clothes followed. Within minutes of unpacking, she had given away most of them. She decided to keep one particularly beautiful and soft blanket for herself. The next morning, Manavati saw her speaking to an old, sickly South Indian man who was obviously very poor. He told Lakshmi that he never stopped feeling cold. Of course, she immediately gave him her blanket.

Manavati also remembers that despite being the regiment commander and a cabinet minister to boot, Lakshmi was never bossy or authoritarian. She was always friendly and affectionate towards all the women soldiers and when they queued up for a meal, plate in hand, she too would do the same.

When the INA headquarters moved to Rangoon, so did the Ranis. Soon they followed other units to the front, where they engaged in actual combat. By this time the tide of war had turned against the Axis powers, and the men and women of the INA stood no chance against the Allies, who fought them on the ground and pounded them mercilessly from the sky. Actually, people like Prem and Lakshmi had not really believed that they would defeat the British militarily, but felt that if only they could enter Indian territory, the people would be inspired to rise up against their colonial masters and drive them out. It is truly tragic that so few people in India have any knowledge or understanding of this unique and inspiring chapter in the history of our freedom struggle.

Prem, along with many other officers and men, was arrested by the British in May 1945. He was brought to Delhi and imprisoned in the Red Fort. In an incredible act of stupidity, the British government decided to publicly try three officers—Prem Sahgal, a Hindu; Shahnawaz, a Muslim; and Gurbaksh Singh Dhillon, a Sikh—at the Red Fort, so that the whole world could be convinced of their treachery. In the emotionally charged atmosphere of the time, when millions of Indians were determined to wait no longer for their freedom, this evoked memories of the trial of the last Mughal emperor, Bahadur Shah Zafar, which was also held in the Red Fort after the British quelled the Great Mutiny of 1857, the first war of Indian Independence. The accused, by virtue of the fact that they represented the three major religious communities of the country at a time when it was being vivisected in the name of religion by wily politicians, aided and abetted by their British rulers, enjoyed a huge tidal wave of public support. This wave did not leave the armed forces untouched and, in all likelihood, infected them with the virus of disloyalty against which the British were desperately trying to create public disgust.

Lakshmi was arrested in July 1945 and kept under house arrest in Rangoon, where she lived with a sympathetic and hospitable Burmese family. Many of the officers of the British army stationed in Rangoon or passing through were, of course, Indians. Many were friends of Lakshmi's family or were, in any case, extremely sympathetic towards her. One of them was Thimayya, the senior-most Indian army officer to pass through Rangoon at the time. He later became the commander-in-chief of the Indian army. An old family friend, he was a constant visitor, much to the consternation of the soldiers who were supposed to be guarding Lakshmi in captivity! Lakshmi was even allowed to practise medicine during this period of very lax captivity. All limits were transgressed, however, when on 21 October she addressed a public meeting commemorating the anniversary of the formation of the Provisional Government of Azad Hind. This event received wide coverage, and the British rulers in India were not amused. Orders were issued for Lakshmi to be transferred to Kalaw, in the interiors. Here too she was given her own house and establishment. Old friends like the Sardar Ishwar Singh family lived nearby, so she was well looked after.

Meanwhile, the Constituent Assembly began its sessions in Delhi. Ammu was an elected member from Dindigul and she, along with many others, pressed for Lakshmi's early release and return to India. Finally, in August 1946, after the Red Fort trial was over, the three accused, first sentenced to hanging and then to transportation for life, were given royal pardon because of popular pressure.

Lakshmi was brought to Calcutta from Rangoon by plane and set free at Dum Dum airport. She did not have a penny in her pocket, but she did have her younger brother Subram's address in the city. She took a taxi and told the driver that her brother would pay the fare. The driver turned around, took a close look at her and said delightedly, 'I will drive you around anywhere you like for as long as you like as my guest!' On reaching Subram's flat, she found it locked. Her sister-in-law had left for Lahore to have a baby, and Subram was on tour. (She later learned that her mother had come to Calcutta from Delhi and had been going to the airport every day for the past ten days, hoping to receive Lakshmi. Finally, she had given up and left for Delhi the previous evening.)

The British officer who had accompanied Lakshmi from Rangoon checked into the Grand Hotel where he met Aurobindo Bose, a relative of Netaji's who seemed to be anxiously looking for someone. He went up to him and said, 'I think I know who you are looking for. You will probably find her at her brother's.' Aurobindo rushed to Subram's flat and found Lakshmi sitting on the steps, looking quite forlorn. He took her to the Bose family home, from where she left for Delhi the next morning.

Prem was also in Delhi and the next few days, weeks and months were hectic and exciting. The INA heroes and heroines were the darlings of the nation, which wanted to do nothing else but fete them. They, however, had serious work to do: hundreds of INA personnel and their families were coming to India sick, wounded and destitute, and the priority was to collect an INA relief fund. While Prem stayed on in Delhi (he was secretary and Jawaharlal Nehru, president, of the relief committee), Lakshmi went to Madras where a huge camp for the INA refugees was set up, and then on to Kerala. Her cousin Susheela remembers the day that Lakshmi arrived in Anakara. From the local railway station she had to cross the dry riverbed to the village, and soon she was at the head of a huge procession of excited men, women and children. Finally, she reached Vadakath House, where her grandmother was waiting for her, tears streaming down her cheeks.

Prem and Lakshmi married in Lahore in March 1947. Rioting, already sporadic, was becoming more bloody and vicious as the mandarins in Delhi drew lines across the map of the subcontinent. They did not stay long, and soon left for Kanpur in Uttar Pradesh where Prem, who was 'unemployable' in what was still British India, had found a job in a textile mill. They did not expect to stay in the hot, dusty town for long, but ended up spending the rest of their lives there.

While many rejoiced on 15 August, Prem, Lakshmi and many of their INA friends were heartbroken. Their interest in politics had turned cynical, and they became more and more involved with their professions. Lakshmi had more than enough on her plate, attending to the Punjabi refugees that came streaming into Kanpur, as also to the women members of the city's large Muslim population that was no longer welcomed by most of the Hindu doctors.

Soon they had two daughters, a hectic social life which included tennis parties and amateur dramatics alongside hours devoted to welfare activities. Then in 1971, millions of refugees from East Bengal streamed into India. Lakshmi joined a medical camp at the border run by the People's Relief Committee, which had strong affiliations to the CPI(M) in West Bengal. The tireless devotion and commitment of her colleagues made a strong impression on her, and long discussions with them soon erased her anger about the Communists' mistaken understanding of Netaji and his strategies for winning independence. After returning to Kanpur, Lakshmi became a CPI(M) member and was active first in the trade unions and then in the All India Democratic Women's Association (AIDWA), in which many women party members worked.

During the anti-Sikh riots that engulfed many parts of the country after the assassination of Prime Minister Indira Gandhi by her security guards, Lakshmi stood outside her small clinic in an area which had many Sikh residents and Sikh-owned shops, holding a *chappal* in her hand. With it she threatened armed rioters and looters, and such was the awe in which she was held—and also because so many of them had probably been brought into the world by her— that successive waves of them turned tail and there was not a single casualty in the area. Nor was any home or shop attacked.

In the days when Lakshmi had started her practice in the refugee camps in Kanpur, she had been joined by a young Sikh woman, a *dai* by training, who was always known as Bibiji. She stayed with Lakshmi till the end of her life and lived in three rooms next to the clinic with her family. After she died, her son Kartar continued to live there with his wife and son. By 1984, his wife had died and Kartar had become a disgruntled malcontent on the brink of alcoholism. Thinking that this would be a way to make some easy money, he filed a case of eviction against Lakshmi and went around telling people that once he had got rid of her and her clinic, he would sell the place for a lot of money. Once the rioting started, a large group of people surrounded my mother's clinic and shouted for Kartar Singh to come outside. They told my mother that they were angry about the fact that he had dared to file a case against her and were now going to teach him a lesson. My mother came out and faced them in her trademark pugnacious fashion, and asked them why they had not done this a few weeks or months ago. She proceeded to abuse and berate them until they left. She then put Kartar Singh and his son into the back seat of her car and took them home where, along with more than thirty other Sikhs, they were able to get through the next few days of arson and rioting in complete safety.

After the riots were over, a Sikh organization wanted to 'honour' Lakshmi for her courage. When they approached her she thought the whole thing was very amusing—specially as many political leaders who had behaved shamefully and even criminally during the riots were also being 'honoured'. Needless to say, she refused to have anything to do with all of this.

Lakshmi combined active political work and her work in the AIDWA, of which she was the founding vice-president, with total commitment to the medical profession and her calling as a doctor to the poor. She participated in various working class struggles and strikes, and was invariably the first to arrive at the mill gate for picketing.

In 2002, Lakshmi was the joint Left candidate for the post of President of India, the first woman to run for office. Her campaign was unique for the enthusiasm that it generated, even though there was no chance of her winning. 'Just like the INA,' she said. 'We may have lost the battle but we did win the war for independence, and something like that is going to happen again!'

At close to ninety, she still practises medicine, treating the poor, fighting against globalization which is making medicines expensive and crippling public health services, and against the Hindutva fanatics who fill her with disgust and abhorrence. She was in Bombay for the celebrations of the 50th anniversary of the Quit India Movement, and when the Shiv Sena chief minister of Maharashtra tried to touch her feet she quickly put her feet up on the sofa and said 'Don't you touch me with your bloodstained hands!' An enthusiastic political activist, she can think of her life only in terms of service to those in need.

Breaking the Status Quo

Shikha Trivedy

When the Bahujan Samaj Party chief, Kanshi Ram, first met Mayawati, he asked her what she wanted to do in her life. 'I want to become a district collector,' replied Mayawati. It was around this time that Kanshi Ram declared his intention of endorsing Mayawati as the leader who would one day occupy the highest positions of power in India, from where she could order the most senior officers in the IAS to do her bidding. 'When I became chief minister of UP for the first time in 1995,' she says with pride, 'and Kanshi Ram saw top-ranking bureaucrats queuing up in front of me with files in their hands, he had tears in his eyes. It was one of the happiest moments of his life and I experienced, for the first time, the immense power that a politician wields.'

Mayawati likes to repeat this story. She seems to have made this experience the pivot of her life, a life from which she appears to have erased the past and the personal to reach the pinnacle of success with just one goal—to capture political power. Her political life, she believes, *is* her private life; her only life, dedicated to her people, the Dalits. That she is the undisputed leader of the Dalits in India's most populous and politically influential state, Uttar Pradesh (UP), is undeniable.

Mayawati has learnt the art of survival. Whether it has taken a toll on her personal life is impossible to know, as she has never revealed her true feelings and emotions. During one meeting in which I tried to go beyond her public face, she was impatient and short with me. 'You have often confessed your love for nature. Do you like the mountains or the sea?' I asked. Her reply: 'I don't have the time to go for a walk in the mountains or a stroll on the beach. I have never visited a wildlife sanctuary. Looking at the new flowers in my garden gives me all the pleasure I want from nature.' When I asked her if she likes music, she reacted with contempt. 'I even dislike the sound of the birds which come and make such a noise outside my window every morning. I am constantly asking my servants to scare them away. When I am alone, I am either thinking or writing my speeches. Sometimes I keep a diary and make notes in it about what I have seen or heard that day. I don't like to be disturbed.'

'Which was the last film you saw?'

'I don't remember. It was a long time ago. Before I joined politics. I don't have time for all these frivolous things.'

'Have you ever watched a cricket match?'

'I have no interest in sports.'

'Do you read at all?'

'Only books written by Babasaheb Ambedkar. I also like to read about the leaders of the bahujan samaj, their struggles and their contribution to the upliftment of our people.'

'So what do you do in your free time?'

'I have no free time.'

I have been told that Mayawati prefers white upholstery to any other colour, and is obsessive about cleanliness and punctuality. She will not allow people to enter her house with their slippers on, fearing they might bring in germs and bacteria. 'To run an organization it is essential to be neat in one's personal habits, to have an uncluttered mind, and to instil a sense of order in the people around you.' When asked how often she met her family, she replied saying: 'I have no time. I definitely see them once an year, on my birthday.'

Mayawati was born in New Delhi on 15 January 1956 into a middle class family of Jatavs, who were traditionally known as Chamars or leather workers. Her father had moved to the capital from Badalpur, a village in western UP, after he got a government job as a clerk in the telecommunications department. The family prospered when they started a milk dairy and Mayawati, with her six brothers and two sisters, led an unexceptional middle class existence.

Mayawati had always wanted to rise above her caste limitations and become someone important on the Indian political landscape. In 1977, she is said to have hijacked a public meeting in Delhi which was called to discuss the problems of the scheduled castes in the country. She aggressively opposed the veteran socialist and Janata Party maverick Raj Narain, who had referred to them as Harijans. News of her spirited stand reached Kanshi Ram who was, at the time, an unknown Dalit leader. 'He met me and persuaded me to join him in his fight for social justice,' she said, and thus became her mentor.

In 1978, Kanshi Ram founded the Backward and Minority Communities' Employees Fund (BAMCEF), an all India organization of government employees, in an effort to fight caste discrimination. It gave him both a dedicated cadre of educated men as well as a source of funds through their donations. Most of the members belonged to the Chamar community, which in post-Independence India prospered more than any other Dalit caste from the north. They made their money in the leather business, and were the first to be educated and benefit from the reservation policies of the

Congress government. A white-collar middle class had emerged from among the members of this community, and Mayawati's family was part of it.

BAMCEF'S appeal broadened in 1982 with the formation of the Dalit Shoshit Samaj Sangharsh Samiti (DS4), which tried to establish its presence in villages through agitations, protests and mass demonstrations. Mayawati, armed with a lawyer's degree, gave up her job as a school teacher and joined the *sangarsh*. She instantly became a close aide of Kanshi Ram's, having recognized that as his *shagird* she could be launched into a successful career in politics. It caused resentment in the ranks, but did not lead to any revolt in a movement that, at the time, was essentially a one man show. Only Kanshi Ram could take decisions—everyone else had to take orders. When the Bahujan Samaj Party (BSP) was formed in 1984 to give political expression to BAMCEF and DS4, Mayawati was there by Kanshi Ram's side.

A new era of caste-based mobilization was about to take place in UP that would, for the first time since Independence, disconnect the Dalits from upper-caste mainstream parties—primarily the Congress—and propel them on to the centrestage of Indian politics armed with a party, ideology and identity. Kanshi Ram was clear from the start that the BSP, unlike other Dalit organizations, was not a reform movement but a political force first, whose aim was to attain power and use it to improve the lives of the Dalits. In fact, on more than one occasion, he contrasted the BSP with the Ambedkarite parties of Maharashtra, claiming that the latter had been co-opted all too easily by the ruling political establishment. Kanshi Ram's singular approach suited Mayawati's temperament, ambition and style of working perfectly.

Between 1985 and 1989 the BSP did not win any

elections, but its vote base began to grow beyond the educated Dalits who lived in India's towns and cities. Mayawati lost two by-elections to the Lok Sabha, from Bijnore and Hardwar, in 1985 and 1987. Finally, in 1989, she made her parliamentary debut. But her real goal was to be the chief minister of UP, and she was in a hurry. The BSP knew that it would have to start looking beyond its scheduled caste vote bank to achieve a national presence, and in the early 1990s the party tried to mobilize OBCs, SCs, STs and other minority groups on to a common platform of *bahujans*, overcoming caste, class and religious differences. There are 60 scheduled caste and 58 OBC groups in UP, out of which 21 are Muslim. Nearly 50 per cent of them are landless labourers or marginal farmers.

In 1991, despite the BJP's sweeping victory in UP on the Ayodhya issue, the BSP managed to hold its own when other political forces in the state were virtually wiped out. But it was only in the 1993 elections that the BSP came into its own—the party had successfully positioned itself as a secular, lower caste party, and massive Dalit participation in the polls ensured that it was destined to play a major role in UP politics.

A Samajwadi Party-BSP coalition government was formed which gave the identity of the bahujan samaj a central place. However, it lasted only sixteen months, as opposing class interests and rivalry over the same social base led to a steady deterioration in the relationship between the two coalition partners. Clashes between the supporters of chief minister Mulayam Singh Yadav and Mayawati became commonplace, and the two became sworn enemies. As the BSP withdrew its support to that government in 1995, Mayawati claimed that Mulayam's men had confined and besieged her when she was at the State Guest House in Lucknow. She was locked in for hours before being airlifted to the Raj Bhavan, where she was administered the oath of office as chief minister in the dead of the night. Her ally this time was the BJP.

Mayawati has always seen the State Guest House incident as an attack not just on a political rival, but on a Dalit and a woman. She has never forgotten this episode, and it is this enmity that has continued to define caste politics in UP from that moment onwards. Every time Mayawati came back to power she would make it a point to cut Mulayam down to size by slapping criminal cases against him and his party men. It became a pattern, and the Yadav chieftain returned the favour when he came to power in 2003, signalling an end to any possibility of an OBC-Dalit alliance in UP.

Vendetta politics has widened the divide between the Yadavs, who dominate the Samajwadi Party, and the Dalit supporters of the BSP. This sentiment was widely articulated throughout UP after Mulayam Singh Yadav announced that he was disbanding seven of the thirteen new districts created by Mayawati during her tenure as chief minister in 1997, all of which were named after Dalit symbols: Mahatma Jyotiba Phule Nagar, Kaushambi, Gautam Buddha Nagar, Shravasti, Shahuji Maharaj Nagar, Sant Kabirdas Nagar and Mahamayanagar.

'In Mayawati's reign, statues of Dalit icons were consecrated across UP's landscape.' This was what the Dalits said to establish their role in the cultural heritage of the country. Naming roads, towns and institutions after leaders was only a way of ensuring that history records their existence and contribution.

Ironically, neither Mayawati nor Mulayam Singh Yadav seem interested in reviving the memory of those heroes who could genuinely have united their constituents. It is no surprise, as their separate political identities can only be sustained if the caste divisions remain. Instead of broadening a pro-poor alliance, the BSP chose to enter a new phase of bahujan samaj politics that revolved around coalition building with upper caste parties, primarily the BJP. Perhaps because the BSP had never aimed for a revolutionary transformation of the existing system, social or economic, it was able to enter into a political alliance with the BJP, which it earlier identified as an enemy.

The last time Mayawati became chief minister of UP (in 2002), I travelled across the state to find out what her people and partners thought of the arrangement. I found that a number of Mayawati's core Dalit supporters did not appreciate the alliance with the BJP. The BSP's greatest strength had been that it gave Dalits an identity of their own and a feeling of self worth. The alliance with the BJP led to a questioning of that sense of pride. For example, in a Jatav basti on the outskirts of Lucknow, a woman who lives without electricity and safe drinking water complained, 'We have nothing. No ration cards, no sanitation. Whatever grants come to the village are cornered by the upper castes and corrupt government officials. We cannot survive on pride alone . . . What does it matter that a Dalit is the chief minister of UP when she has done so little to improve our lives?'

Outside a primary school we saw a statue of Dr Ambedkar which had been knocked off its pedestal on to the ground. The villagers told us that Mayawati had not been able to protect the most popular and widespread expression of Dalit pride. The statues were routinely vandalized in villages whose panchayats were controlled by the BSP's then partner, the BJP. The teacher of the school was reluctant to speak to us. Hesitatingly, she said in a scared tone, 'In this area, wherever they have put up an Ambedkar statue it has led to violence, because sometimes upper caste goondas break his hand; sometimes his leg. Our village is dominated by Brahmins. We have decided that it is better not to put up Babasaheb's statue because whenever something like this happens we feel terrible. But we are helpless, and cannot protect him.'

Ironically, in the capital, Lucknow, just a few kilometres away, the BJP was exhibiting great keenness to incorporate Ambedkar into the pantheon of Hindutva heroes. Vinay Katiyar, the BJP president in the state at the time, was dismissive of the BSP's claim to represent the Ambedkar legacy. 'No one can have a patent on a great leader. Our party has a large number of Dalits. We have made a Dalit the chief minister of UP. It's only after we put our lotus in the mouth of their elephant that Ganesh was created. Mayawati is in power today because of our generosity.'

Every political party wanted to use Dr Ambedkar as a symbol to gather votes, but few had use for his message.

The years of the BJP-BSP alliance, in some sense, signalled an end to the agitation-based politics of the BSP and the beginning of an election-oriented movement. This was also reflected in Mayawati's strategy of putting up more candidates from other castes, both 'backward' and 'forward', as well as other minorities to broaden her party's base. The strategy paid off, but it was apparent that the people who were voted to power on the slogan of Dalit empowerment did very little for them.

In a small village I went to, there were two schools. A two-room building, falling to pieces, where the students sat on the floor, was the government school where the Dalits sent their children. Down the road, a newly-built private institution was attended mostly by the children of Kurmis, a powerful backward caste group of the area. It was built by the MLA and the MP, both Kurmis. Both had won on BSP tickets.

The principal of the government school told us that Dalit children came to school only to collect their scholarships or for food; otherwise they worked in people's homes or in the fields. They could not afford to study, let alone spend the money to attend private schools.

Mayawati's attempt to widen the social base of her party and capture power with the help of other communities has upset her people. 'The BSP knows,' says a village pradhan, 'that we are a captive vote bank. Our vote will not go to anyone else but them. However, since they need the support of other castes to win a seat, no Dalit is ever given a ticket. We have no stake in the politics of the area.'

Mayawati continued with her winning strategy, and once again distributed tickets across caste lines in the 2002 UP assembly elections. It paid rich dividends. The BSP got 98 seats, up from their previous tally of 66. With no other party getting a clear majority in the UP assembly, she once again became the key player and secured the chief minister's chair by tying up with the BJP. Mayawati's time in government saw her become even more aggressive in pushing for a greater slice of the political cake. It was during this period that allegations of mass-scale corruption and the sale of BSP election tickets to the highest bidder surfaced. Mayawati was implicated in the Taj corridor case, in which she was accused of flouting all norms by allowing a shopping complex to come up around the Taj Mahal.

Worried that the BJP-led NDA government at the centre would use the case to target her, Mayawati decided to pull the plug on her alliance government in UP in late 2003. It was a move that rebounded on her, and several BSP MLAs, mainly Muslims and those from non-Dalit castes, defected and joined hands with Mulayam Singh Yadav. It revealed the limitations of her support base, and proved that many of these MLAs had no individual loyalty to the BSP. It displayed the amoeba-like character of the BSP—a party that splinters easily when it loses office, the lure of power being the only glue that holds it together.

Mayawati emerged seemingly unfazed from all this, keeping all her political options open.

At the Centre she has broken bread with Sonia Gandhi and the UPA alliance, but in Uttar Pradesh she walks alone. She has even been willing to reach out to the BJP once again, but as an astute politician she realizes that her political promiscuity cannot be at the cost of a further dilution of the BSP's Dalit agenda.

She has tried to bring about a new social order using state power, single-mindedly pursuing Dalit-oriented policies in the fields of education, social welfare, employment generation and health, often at the expense of other caste groups. She launched the Ambedkar Rozgar Yojna to provide work for Dalits—50 per cent of the outlay went towards health and family planning, and was reserved for this group alone. Villages with a large concentration of Dalits were identified as 'Ambedkar villages' and were developed on a priority basis. But the reality was that many of her policies only angered the state's predominantly upper caste bureaucracy and the moment she lost power, the bureaucrats hit back—Mayawati's schemes were reversed.

Across western UP, the bureaucracy busily rewrote the script for social justice. In Pithona, a short distance from Agra, Mayawati's fall proved costly for its Jatav population. Pithona had been classified as an Ambedkar village, as more than half its inhabitants were Dalits. When Mayawati was in power the people here got free electricity connections. But with her out of office they were asked to pay one hundred rupees for a connection. When they protested the officers said to them, 'Your government is gone, so who will you complain to?' They also allege that their children are no longer receiving the scholarship money that is due to them.

In the upper caste mohallas of these Ambedkar villages, the mood is different. With Mayawati out of power, there is a sense of anticipation that some benefits may now come the way of the upper castes. In Ladamada, the Thakurs show us the overflowing gutters outside their homes which no one has bothered to clean. They point towards roads that have never been repaired. They claim that only the Jatavs have benefited in this village, and nothing has been done for the rest of the community. Development, they argue, revolves around whichever caste is in power.

During her stints as chief minister, Mayawati had suspended and publicly humiliated several senior government officials for neglecting development work in Ambedkar villages—now it was their turn to get even.

And yet the Ambedkarization of UP, propelled by Mayawati, cannot be wished away. Today schools, libraries, parks and roads across the state have been named after him. His birthday is celebrated with great fervour. Every Dalit, educated or illiterate, knows who Ambedkar was and what he did for them.

In a further effort to nurture the growth of a Dalit identity, Ravidas and Valmiki temples were built, and statues of Dalit leaders were installed throughout the state. The BSP urged its supporters to learn from the teachings and lives of Shahuji Maharaj, Jyotiba Phule, Periyar and other such Dalit icons. A new pantheon of heroes and heroines like Jhalkari Bai, Uda Devi, Bijli Pasi and Matadin Hela was created as the BSP delved into the past to collect as many symbols as they could to give the Dalits a sense of history.

Much of this identity building was Kanshi Ram's doing, and came from personal experience. He had faced discrimination for being a Dalit, and wanted to make it possible for his people to live with respect. There is a story about the time when he came up with the idea of putting up statues of Dalit personalities. He was asked to decide what image he would prefer to cast them in. Kanshi Ram is said to have laid out the calendar images of all the Sikh gurus in front of the artist, and told him to combine their best features to create new images.

Kanshi Ram probably also realized that Mayawati could never completely identify with the suffering and humiliation that Dalits faced, perhaps because she had never known it herself. Since she could not mobilize people by being a victim, he chose to make her a heroic figure instead, surrounding her with symbols of valour. This included statues of women like Jhalkari Bai, a Kori who disguised herself as Rani Laxmibai of Jhansi and helped her queen escape from the British, or Uda Devi, the courageous wife of a local Pasi chief who was killed fighting the British in Lucknow during the Mutiny of 1857. The idea was to link Mayawati with the brave subaltern heroines of the past.

In the process, a subtle shift took place within the BSP political hierarchy. During the time that Kanshi Ram was still the leader of the BSP, Mayawati kept her ambitions in check, but as his health began to fail she was ready to take a step forward. In 2002, Kanshi Ram virtually anointed Mayawati his successor. The transition of power was instantly reflected in the visual propaganda of the BSP—the towering figure of Kanshi Ram made way for a supremely confident image of Mayawati. While Jayalalithaa was often depicted on hoardings alongside her mentor even after his death, body turned towards him and hands folded in a gesture of respect, Mayawati stopped sharing this space almost immediately. However, her speeches still contained references to Kanshi Ram, whose name she always prefixes with 'manyawar' (respected) in a public gesture of reverence.

Unlike Jayalalithaa, who successfully exploited her mass popularity as a beautiful film actress as well as her closeness to the superstar chief minister MGR, or Sonia Gandhi, whose political career is linked to what the political scientist Ali A. Mazrui calls the phenomenon of 'female accession to male martyrdom' after Rajiv Gandhi's assassination, Mayawati rose from the ranks. Her rise is not unlike that of Mamata Banerjee, who emerged as a student leader fighting the Left in West Bengal, or Uma Bharti, whose political journey began as a rabble-rouser for the saffron brotherhood.

Although Mayawati possesses neither the charisma of Jayalalithaa, the political heritage of Sonia Gandhi, the oratorical skills of Uma Bharti, or even the agitation-based style of Mamata Banerjee, what she does have is single-minded ambition, which requires no props. This has also prevented her from being manipulated by male politicians both within and outside the party. She has avoided the fate of someone like Uma Bharti, whose bosses in the BJP looked on approvingly when she applauded the demolition of the Babri Masjid, or more recently when she resigned as chief minister of Madhya Pradesh, but dumped her when she trashed their shortcomings publicly.

Mayawati works alone—she has no advisers and believes

that she does not need any. She is the sole leader of the BSP and is responsible for devising its strategy and managing the collection and disbursement of party funds. People who have been thrown out of the BSP over the years have said in interviews that she brooks no opposition. You can only survive in the BSP, they say, if you can cope with the possibility of public humiliation and her legendary arrogance.

As her birthday celebrations become bigger and more ostentatious with each passing year, the charges of corruption become sharper. Ensconced in a palatial house in South Delhi, it almost seems as if she is using the power of money to challenge age-old hierarchies. Mayawati's response to all this criticism has been to ignore it. It is almost as if she believes that if injustice is the way of life then what the upper castes can do, she can do better. She has often asked angrily, 'Why does everyone raise such a hue and cry if my people observe my birthday as Swabhiman Diwas? Is Nehru's birthday not remembered as Children's Day? Don't other politicians have birthday parties in five star hotels? Why should I be singled out? Because I am a Dalit and I should be kept in my place?' Each time she is accused of a misdeed, she immediately interprets it as a larger conspiracy against the Dalit people.

But is Mayawati a modern woman politician, or a just a shrewd politician who happens to be a woman? Had she seen herself as a woman politician, she would not have hesitated to give her gender a robust identity like she has given to the Dalits. The BSP would have had more elected women representatives at all levels, and her time as chief minister of UP would have made a difference to the health, education and welfare of her female voters. This has not happened. Women as individuals have no place as yet in her political or even social scheme of things.

I would have been readily convinced that Mayawati the politician has left no space for Mayawati the woman, but for two things. The first is her appearance. Mayawati may have discarded her long hair (which she once tied in a girlish pony-tail) for a short, no-nonsense haircut that makes her look stern and masculine, she may have rejected her shimmering, gold embroidered saris for the more functional salwar kameez, but she continues to wear feminine colours—shades of pink, peach and orange, colours her people can identify with. Mayawati has almost never been seen in white, a colour associated with the upper castes and their notions of sacredness and purity. She still flaunts her passion for jewellery—in the earlier days her preference was for gold, but that has now been replaced by diamonds.

The second is Mayawati's relationship with Kanshi Ram. When she was asked about it several years ago she simply replied, 'We live together. He needs someone to look after him.' They have continued to live together despite allegations from Kanshi Ram's family that he is a prisoner in her house. Mayawati says they are innocent people who are being manipulated by her enemies, but somewhere the hurt remains. A similar charge was made by an interviewer on a television show. Why didn't she ever allow anyone to meet her ailing mentor? Mayawati marched into his room, cameras following her every move. She stroked his head affectionately, patted his cheek, asked him how he was feeling and what he would like to eat, fussing over him like a mother.

She was not at ease in this role, and did not try and hide it. Mayawati has said in the past that Kanshi Ram treated her like his son, and it was evident that she was only doing her duty by taking care of him in his old age.

In the Hindu context it is possible for a woman to be

powerful and aggressive. Shyama Nandan Mishra compared Indira Gandhi to the goddess Durga after the 1971 war against Pakistan. This is how Mayawati would like to be perceived. At a public meeting in Ahmedabad she exhorted the crowds to think of her as their goddess, to donate to her party all the offerings they would have made to temples.

Mayawati has ensured that a statue of her has been installed next to one of her mentor, Kanshi Ram. When she unveiled them she remarked, 'Who knows whether they will be put up after we are gone. For now at least the new generations of Dalits will never forget us.'

They almost certainly won't.

Revival and Restoration

Jaya Jaitly

It is difficult to describe a woman who gave a new lease of life to folk theatre, handicrafts and handmade textiles in India, was a colossus on the political stage, yet was so private that in her autobiography she fails to share the names of two of the major influences in her life—her mother and grandmother. She married the remarkable poet and theatre personality Harendranath Chattopadhyay, with whom she brought about innovative changes in stage productions, but chooses not to talk about him or why they parted company after some years. While she talks about her work with her husband in the world of theatre, she deliberately avoids elaborate descriptions of him and does not reveal her view of his personality and contributions; neither does the memoir reveal any of the joys, intimacies or discord in the course of their relationship as husband and wife. Kamaladevi Chattopadhyay was a magnificent woman who remains an enigma. Beautiful, aesthetic, creative and humane, she could also be cold, intensely private, distant and brusque with those who wasted her time. 'Whatever the modern trend may be,' she writes, 'I do not think in a life story one is required to lower the barriers of the discreet reticence which governs our everyday life and affairs.' To avoid being intrusive by excessively delving into what she kept private, we need to go over her life 'like a landscape touched with patches of light and shadows as the day passes over it', just as she would have wished.

As a young girl, Kamala's life in Karnataka was full of festivals and flowers. She belonged to a culture in which guests were greeted with flowers before they were served tea or coffee, and weaving flower garlands was the high point for young girls during celebrations and festivals. Dressing up in long silk skirts and adorning themselves with jewellery, taking part in rituals like performing the 'marriage' of the tulsi plant in the month of Shravan, lighting little boat-lamps made from banana leaves at Makarasankranti, or merely experiencing the exhilarating monsoon rains in the month of Ashad taught Kamala the link between lifestyle, ritual, food and celebration. Paper lanterns were made by everyone in the family, not bought in the market where festivals became commercial propositions rather than occasions of personal involvement. Kamaladevi delighted in these occasions, which instilled in her an abiding understanding of Indian creativity and aesthetics, as well as a deeper understanding of the value of indigenous craftsmanship. The beauty and art of handmade things was a firsthand experience for her, and these childhood pursuits that many forget in the cynicism and sophistication of adulthood later motivated her to establish institutions and recommend policies for the betterment of craftspeople. For her they were treasures with which to transform independent India's attitudes towards its handcrafted products and ancient skills and traditions. Throughout her life she continued to embroider embellishments on to the edges of her saris or adorn herself with flowers, trinkets and glass bangles, even when she was over eighty years old. She carried this interest outside herself to locate, nurture and preserve the multitudes of craft skills in India, and put the spotlight on the people who practised them.

Kamaladevi Dhareshwar, as she was born on 3 April 1903, was fortunate in the circumstances of her birth and family background. She belonged to an upper caste Saraswat Brahmin family which owned five acres of land and a large bungalow. It was an aristocratic family which believed in aesthetic cultural practices and high thinking. It was unusually progressive in its ideas of women's awareness and emancipation and encouraged education, particularly for women, based on ideas, involvement and debate. Kamaladevi's mother was bold and fearless, and was determined to provide her daughter with all the political, social and cultural inputs that were available to men in the early 1900s. She thought nothing of stepping out of her traditional place in the home as a crusader for women's education, and fought against gender discrimination. She was responsible for setting up the first Mahila Sabha, a forum for women, in the region. Kamaladevi's grandmother was a powerful, reticent and highly intellectual woman who gave birth to seven children. She firmly believed in the importance of reading and encouraged Kamaladevi to make books her lifelong companions. As a result, Kamaladevi was exposed to new ideas and discussions on a variety of subjects from a relatively early age. Her mother and grandmother encouraged her to learn several regional languages, practice the discipline of writing, participate in sports and learn music from professional teachers. This kind of upbringing prepared her to absorb all sorts of information on a wide range of subjects with a spirit of inquiry and independence. She was taken to plays and political gatherings, and these opened her mind to the possibilities of a life dedicated towards serving the underprivileged in society. Both her mother and grandmother were unusually fearless women who often travelled alone in the pursuit of their interests and beliefs, unlike others in a society that expected women to stay in the seclusion of their homes, leading genteel lives. It was rare for women to be so liberal in those days, yet the climate of those days was such that society accepted anything done for its betterment, and people raised no questions about their political and social activism.

In Karnataka, small towns and villages had little raised platforms known as *kattas*, from which old texts would be read and bhajans would be sung. People would tell stories and interpret the ancient texts. The gathering spot served as a welcoming and informal community centre. Kamaladevi loved slipping into the katta near her aunt's house to be a part of the goings on. She later mused nostalgically upon these wayfarer's havens as a common shelter that offered warmth, entertainment, education, friendship, or even a place to have a short nap, without the participants needing to establish their identities or bona fides. Modern restaurants or coffee shops were for her a far cry from the real 'food for the soul' that a katta offered freely to anyone who wished to join. Young Kamala's childhood memories created a firm foundation of 'Indianness' that probably helped formulate her nationalistic pursuits, and also gave a deeper meaning to issues like creative community activity, a positive spirit that mingled with the graciousness of living, and an abiding love for the wonders of nature.

Liberalism today allows freedom without necessarily demanding any responsibility towards society. In Kamaladevi's time, while she was encouraged to play tennis with young men, she was also expected to play a role in the development of underprivileged women, take part in political activities, nurture her intellect and widen her experience of life in a serious and dedicated manner.

What can clearly be said of Kamaladevi is that every input she received in her early years, whether positive or negative, was reinvented into creative, constructive and indelible actions that brought honour and hope to others. Her childhood influences can be pulled out like strands, each leading to a set of actions or results that demonstrated her remarkable personality and her multiple contributions right up to the time of her death in 1988. Thus, her early cultural influences led her to pursue the creative expressions of India, her proximity to those involved in the freedom movement led her into politics, and her own family influences made her erudite, articulate and bold in the field of social reform.

Dakshina Kannada, or South Canara, in the southern part of Karnataka, was full of the rituals and ceremonies associated with what are today rather condescendingly termed 'folk' lifestyles. Kamala witnessed a feast of cultural activity that came with the concept of *Bhuta*, a primitive folk belief in the departed spirits of the ancestors. These beliefs gave rise to Bhuta shrines in many villages, dedicated to spirits which could be benefactors, heroic personalities, protectors, or who had the propensity to be mischievous and needed to be propitiated. The Bhuta cult also nourished a vast number of songs, dances and ritual sports like cock fights and buffalo races, in which members of all castes participated. Society had a social and cultural balance, and both the arts and sports received sustenance from the people. Yakshagana plays were performed to appease the Bhutas, and were simple in style and close to the people. Later, they developed into elaborate dance-dramas and are now performed seasonally in Karnataka and Andhra Pradesh, even travelling wider as part of national and international cultural festivals. Kamaladevi's own home was surrounded by rice fields, which when cleared after the harvest became a vast theatre where such folk plays could be performed. This kaleidoscope of creative activity was right at Kamaladevi's doorstep, and laid the foundation for her lifelong involvement with theatre, its crafts, stage settings and performers. Yakshagana was deeply imprinted in Kamaladevi's mind. The name merely means 'a style of music', but the form evolved into dramatic themes, rhythmic footwork and witty extempore dialogues that served as satirical comments on current events. The costumes were elaborate and distinguished the heroes from the villains, fully commanding the attention of the audience to its magnificent presentation.

She grew up appreciating the beauty of the intricate wooden structures that served as Bhuta temples, trances and oracles that took place in the public gaze, and performances full of song and dance that were put up by different castes, expressing their own identity and distinct cultural style. Imagine the awe and wonder the young girl must have felt when exposed to the multifaceted and extraordinary colours of her own culture. It was these early influences that made Kamaladevi a theatre lover for life, not merely as a *rasika*, an aficionado, but a woman who decided to take to acting and travelling across the country with theatre groups to perform before rural and urban audiences. She revelled in examining different schools of acting, both in India and abroad, and spent a considerable part of her youthful years enjoying the company of actors. Before the age of twenty she had married the skilled actor Harendranath Chattopadhyay, whose sister Sarojini Naidu remained Kamaladevi's close friend throughout her politically active period and after. Sarojini Naidu was another great Indian woman who strode the political stage as easily as she wrote lyrical poems. Kamaladevi and Harendranath became popular performers in their travelling company of actors, staging plays in small towns before enthusiastic audiences. During their travels, she once found a pile of wooden Bhuta figures, later assessed to be eight hundred years old, lying neglected and decaying out in the open. She bought them to be displayed in the Crafts Museum in Delhi in exchange for some freshly commissioned pieces that were more suitable for worship. She did this in agreement with the temple authorities, only to find herself in deep trouble with the auditing authorities of the government for having piled up old stuff in exchange for new, and having committed the double crime of not documenting it on paper. To make things worse, some local politicians then accused her of taking away sacred images from ancient temples. As often happens to honest and caring people, she found herself 'a criminal twice over', until the issue was resolved with the help of one of her political colleagues who happened to be a trustee of the temple.

Kamaladevi's fascination with the theatre arts later led her to establish the National Theatre Crafts Museum, which she named after a close colleague, Srinivas Malliah. In the museum she displayed the fabulous ornaments, masks, headgear and costumes of different forms of folk theatre. In a time when the culture of television with its alien images and lifestyles is rapidly detaching younger generations from their own indigenous cultural expressions, such treasures are invaluable to educate them about their roots. Any other country would have adopted this pioneering work and taken it from strength to strength, but instead the theatre museum in New Delhi languishes, brooding over its neglect as the passions and concerns of a new era pass it by.

The museum had been a shared dream of theirs. Those who knew her closely refer to her special relationship with Malliah, a dedicated politician and wealthy businessman who, according to Kamaladevi, resisted getting into the mould expected of most politicians. Described by her as 'a close compatriot' throughout her political career, the generosity of her words for him in her memoirs, the unhesitating admiration for what she believed were his outstanding qualities, his incisive mind, sense of humour, sensitivity to aesthetics, nature and elegance are easily shared with the reader. The two had a deep and abiding friendship which was never damaged by her differences with him on political issues. She even admitted that after his sudden death she was gradually able to better understand the value and accuracy of his political perceptions.

Not many women of that time would have collaborated so closely with a man on public issues and shared a deep personal relationship without awkwardness. It took both confidence and courage. As with all her interactions, whether it was with Gandhi, Nehru or other stalwarts, she never hesitated to disagree with them when she had her own point of view, even while she respected and admired them greatly.

Mahatma Gandhi's strong emphasis on the need to strengthen the rural artisan and his call to take to spinning cotton yarn and wearing khadi naturally found a special resonance in Kamaladevi's heart. She was already attuned to the sensibilities and charms of handwork. Given her family's propensity for converting personal concerns into service in the public interest, it was but natural that she would give her heart and soul to this cause. During her tours of the country she would gather rare artefacts, document natural dyeing processes, identify weavers with special capabilities and encourage her colleagues to take up work with them as a lifelong commitment. For her, each action was a part of a larger action. If the British had to be fought, then western influences needed to be replaced by Indian cultural properties in dress, ornaments, lifestyle accessories and indeed the very textures and colours of everything that went into a home. The Indian identity had to be established with a sound economic base, aesthetic appeal and relevance to national goals. For her these were instruments in a battle against foreign influences, which were crushing India's culture.

Soon after India's independence, Kamaladevi was made chairperson of the All India Handicrafts and Handloom Board. It was an opportunity for her to channel the development of these sectors into a spirit of cultural rejuvenation. During the twenty years that she headed the Handicrafts Board, she was able to establish institutions and systems to assist in the development and marketing of crafts. She established national awards to honour craftspeople who had been economically and socially left by the wayside. The Central Cottage Industries Emporium, considered the flagship store showcasing the handicrafts and handlooms of the country, was initially set up by the Ministry of Commerce upon Jawaharlal Nehru's initiative. When it began running into heavy losses, he suggested it be handed over to the Refugees' Co-operative Union set up by Kamaladevi. Kamaladevi was helped in setting up this union by a group of committed women, including Pupul Jayakar (later Kamaladevi's competitor), Fori Nehru, the wife of Jawaharlal Nehru's cousin B.K. Nehru, and Prem Berry, the wife of a well known dentist in the capital. This elite set created a dynamic and participatory structure that enabled the emporium to blossom into what Nehru later described as a 'modern monument of Delhi like the Qutub of the old era, and a must for visitors'. For many years it set the tone for 'Indianness' in household decor, garments and accessories, combining a high level of aesthetics with a comfortable ambience to shop. Fondly referred to as 'The Cottage', what started as a way of providing some relief and earnings for the Refugees' Co-operative became the first sophisticated department store for India's handicrafts, thanks to Kamaladevi's dedication and efforts.

Kamaladevi Chattopadhyay's early training in writing helped her convert the knowledge she had acquired about crafts into books that detailed fascinating aspects of craft processes and described the particular cultures from which they sprang. These books located and brought alive India's crafts treasures and, for the first time, included the simple, rural, folk crafts and practices that had been overlooked or sought to be destroyed in colonial times. Earlier publications by British scholars or art collectors concentrated on elaborate and expensive objects, fit for kings, but she was particular that the ordinary, everyday object, imbued with the beauty crafted into it by the artisan, should become a part of everyone's lives to elevate the life of the maker and the user out of drabness. The heritage of rural India, from Ladakh to Kerala, Nagaland to Rajasthan, was brought out for the world to see. It would have been easy for a literate and articulate woman like her to rest satisfied with these academic contributions, but the activist in Kamaladevi ensured that she worked on many parallel tracks. She set up a row of emporia in Delhi to sell the handicrafts and handlooms of every state, and was one of the pioneering members of the World Crafts Council. She also founded the All India Design Centre and the Shilpi Kendra in Mumbai. While there were many contenders in the world of politics, a field in which she played an admirable role, it was in the domain of arts and crafts that she stood supreme, as the pioneer and saviour of the innumerable craft traditions of India. Today, in a world full of technology and industrial synthetics, India, like her, stands supreme in the richness of its thriving heritage of hand skills and artistic resources. This would never have happened but for the single-minded perseverance of a woman who combined aesthetics, humanity and politics in a creative and constructive way, nurturing the crushed expressions of India's culture and resuscitating them as a mother would her undernourished children.

Kamaladevi Chattopadhyay, the political woman, emerged unconsciously in a development alongside her cultural interests. Her father's sudden demise when she was a minor brought a drastic change and a huge void in her life. She turned to depend on her maternal uncle (again, she fails to tell us his name in her memoirs), who was well known for his role in the social reform movements stirring in India and the growing agitation for freedom from British rule. He encouraged her to involve herself in his secretarial work and observe and participate in discussions with prominent people like Gopal Krishna Gokhale, Srinivas Shastri, Sir Tej Bahadur Sapru and Sir C. Sankaran Nair, who was known as an iconoclast and differed openly with Mahatma Gandhi on the methods with which to fight British rule.

When her uncle introduced her to C. Rajagopalachari, fondly known as Rajaji, he asked her, 'What are you going to do when you grow up, young lady?' Kamaladevi promptly answered, 'I am going to change society, especially for women.' 'That is a big ambition,' he remarked. 'But I am not afraid,' she retorted. Kamaladevi remembers a gentle pat on her head which she took to be a blessing. Social workers would gather at her uncle's house, drawing Kamaladevi's attention towards serious social change and the political climate necessary to bring it about.

After her uncle's untimely death she was guided by Ramalingam, an old family friend, who saw a restless and capable mind that needed guidance. He initiated her into the world of the co-operative movement which took root in many forms across India. Co-operative societies enabled the working class to organize themselves into self-reliant structures that formed the backbone of their productive and economic activity. The success of the Anand Milk Co-operative in Gujarat and the handloom co-operatives in Tamil Nadu and Andhra Pradesh are well known. They were part of a great movement to inculcate unified activity and encourage self-reliance in the poorest of producers. Within the system of a co-operative the work and profits were equally shared, and collective effort was the ideal. Ramalingam exposed Kamaladevi to conferences of workers, and she discovered in herself a burning desire for social activity that concerned itself with independence and self-reliance.

The social awareness Kamaladevi's mother instilled in her about discrimination against women had expanded into a recognition of the glaring disparities between the different classes of society. She decided to alter her own lifestyle with regard to clothes, the modes of transport she used, and food. While she loved a good meal, the budding socialist in her eventually turned to simplicity and frugality. Also, education in a convent had given her a sense of discipline and austerity that she felt helped her face many trials along the way. Her realization that an unequal social hierarchy and a lack of economic justice would prevent India from the true benefits of freedom spurred her to work on many fronts at the same time. It also prepared her well for the time she would have to spend in jail for participating in the freedom struggle.

Very few people, let alone a woman from a fairly comfortable, middle class background, used to travelling with ease anywhere in the world, would have attempted the Herculean task of rehabilitating the millions of refugees who who were rendered homeless after the bloody partition of India and Pakistan. She was determined that this was not to be a 'relief' effort of handing out blankets and food, but a far greater one of enabling people to build their own futures by first building their own township. She had to fight red tape and resistance to new ideas by a bureaucracy that did not want to share its power and authority: after all, self-help meant no reliance on government largesse. It needed a visionary like Kamaladevi to think differently and use her extraordinary qualities of perseverance and leadership to persuade people who had lived lives of luxury and stability to put aside their trauma to dig the earth with their own hands and construct their own houses, lay roads, cultivate vegetable gardens, set up schools, dispensaries and all the other needs of daily life. The men nearly revolted until the women refugees stepped forward and agreed to get to work. Despite a million difficulties, the first crop of vegetables her refugees cultivated impressed Pandit Nehru, and he arranged for irrigation facilities to link Okhla and Chattarpur for their benefit. Thus emerged the township of Faridabad, just outside Delhi, as a result of her dogged and amazing persistence. The entire job was handled by the Indian Co-operative Union, which was set up by Kamaladevi. Private engineers guided them and friends provided the support that the government was reluctant to give. Not only did the township come up with all the amenities needed for a self-contained existence, but the refugees set up their own little businesses and factories, having learned the spirit of labour and co-operation along the way. The doughty Kamaladevi pursued everyone in the government relentlessly, and would not let those who needed help sit idle until they had achieved what they had set out to do. It would be hard to find a parallel in present times, a woman who took on such an immense ideological and practical task merely because she believed in herself and in her ideas about the benefit of people's rights. The Faridabad of today is a grotesque mutation of her vision, and has turned into everything that is contrary to it. The lands and assets were later sold to higher bidders, who took over the well-planned facilities with a completely different intent. Today, hardly anyone would know that a lone woman inspired by Gandhi's idea of co-operative endeavours had bullied Nehru, motivated dispirited souls, demonstrated a new strategy for development, and set up the entire township of Faridabad against all odds. She lived to see its tragic and ugly transformation and the shattering of her hopes in a new ideal, but this does not alter the fact that only a true leader and visionary could have attempted such a task in the first place.

With her mother as her mentor, the young Kamaladevi had been exposed to the great churnings within the Indian political scene. At fourteen she had listened to a speech by Annie Besant, who had just been elected president of the Indian National Congress. Besant had given up her life in the West and devoted herself to India's social and political journey towards becoming an independent and self-reliant country. Kamaladevi's mother wanted Annie Besant to be an example for her daughter to follow. In her early years she also had occasion to interact closely with Margaret Cousins, the educationist and political activist, who also worked with Annie Besant. She spent hours in the company of Rabindranath Tagore, Maharishi Karve, his wife Anasuya, Verrier Elwin and Pandita Ramabai.

'The past nestles in the present as the future burgeons forth from it,' she wrote, expressing how tradition, creativity and progress were all part of a continuum that elated her. Thus emerged the political Kamaladevi Chattopadhyay—a socialist in practice, a nationalist in fervour, an aesthete in sensibility, and a political worker in action. Here was a self-assured, adult Kamaladevi who was irretrievably moulded into a fearless and multifaceted woman symbolizing a modern, engaged and politically committed human being.

It was a time when politics had not yet become a dirty word among the Indian middle class. The freedom movement in India gave rise to great leaders, but as usual, the women among them are seldom recognized by history. Most of them, such as Sarojini Naidu, Mridula Sarabhai, Ammu Swaminathan and Madame Bhikaji Cama belonged to families that were socially and economically comfortable. However, when they committed themselves to the freedom struggle, they thought nothing of plunging into actions that took them to jail or earned them lathi blows from the police. Kamaladevi put her love for acting to one side and became a member of the Seva Dal, an organization of young volunteers that took charge of the arrangements during major conferences of the Congress Party. Here, too, aesthetics came into play when she dressed the women's brigade in bright orange saris instead of their sombre dark blue ones. On another occasion, while attending a conference in Europe with Sarojini Naidu, the duo discovered that India was not represented with a flag. With the ingenuity and unselfishness typical of women, they happily tore up their saris to make a flag to flutter along with those of other countries.

When she was just twenty-three years old, Margaret Cousins, whom Kamaladevi and others fondly called Gretta, persuaded her to contest a seat in the Madras State Provincial Legislature, which had changed its rules to allow women to become members. With no previous experience in electioneering, she agreed to contest as an Independent and left the arrangements to Margaret Cousins. Kamaladevi lost by just 55 votes, but it brought her into the mainstream of political involvement. A year later, at twenty-four, she formally joined the Congress Party and once again took up the 'broom and basket' tasks of organizing volunteers for major party conferences. Genuine political commitment called for such work at the junior-most level, irrespective of one's background and educational level. Kamaladevi's contributions stood out—she was only twenty-five when she was elected to the All India Congress Committee. When Kamaladevi was asked by Sarojini Naidu to take on the post of secretary of the All India Women's Conference, she panicked and declined. Sarojini Naidu stopped her short saying, 'Don't be silly now. Did you not want to be a social worker, and here when your services are being sought, you refuse. You'd better accept it.' And that was that.

She toured the frontier provinces with Khan Abdul Ghaffar Khan and was feted by the fierce Afridi tribes along the Khyber Pass because she was his friend. She also played an admirable role as a floor whip in the Congress session presided over by Subhash Chandra Bose. She was deeply troubled by Mahatma Gandhi's un-Gandhian treatment of Bose's leadership and the way he chose to undermine his authority. She demanded that Mahatma Gandhi send out a specific message to women to participate in the Salt March, but later regretted questioning his commitment to women in political roles. She was witness to the historic action of Bhagat Singh, and was in the Central Assembly when he let off his 'bomb' and showered leaflets on the gathering. She described Bhagat Singh as a handsome young man with a distracted air that day. She almost openly challenged Nehru and Gandhi on the issue of the wording of the party resolution on Bhagat Singh, as they wanted to disassociate the party from his violence. She believed he should not have been categorized with ordinary terrorists. Kamaladevi often challenged Jawaharlal Nehru into helping her achieve her goals, as she believed that leaders were there to serve the people, but on this matter she desisted after an intense discussion with Acharya Kripalani, one of the most highly respected Congress leaders of the time.

In 1936, Kamaladevi was elected to the post of president of the Congress Socialist Party, which differed ideologically from the Congress Party. They chose to work as a separate group within it rather than divide the party at a time of struggle. She was also the president of the Mangalore District Socialist Party, and officiated the induction of George Fernandes into the party at that time. A young Fernandes had just abandoned life in the seminary, been thrown out of his home and been befriended by the Socialists. In the Socialist Party she worked with stalwarts like Jayaprakash Narayan, Minoo Masani, Ram Manohar Lohia and Yusuf Meherally. The socialists had become disappointed with Nehru's attitudes and strategies, despite his positive responses to their position on many issues.

After the failure of the Round Table talks in London, a general crackdown on all freedom fighters was imminent. Kamaladevi was arrested at Borivili station in Bombay as she was going off to organize a Seva Dal training camp. Getting arrested and going to jail during the freedom movement was a unique experience for a middle class Indian woman like Kamaladevi. She was booked under the Vagrants Act as a person 'without any ostensible means of livelihood and a source of danger to society', and therefore placed in a 'C' class prison. There she led a revolt, listing a host of grievances against the jail administration. The main one was about the quality of underwear apparel provided to the prisoners! As further punishment she was sent into separate barracks where, to her relief, she found Gandhi's close associate Mira Behn. Later, she was in the Yerwada Women's Prison. At every such occasion she delighted in the company of senior women political leaders and believed that such experiences helped sharpen her resolve in the struggle for freedom.

It was all the more remarkable that she gave up political activity after India attained freedom, and refused various political appointments that came her way.

Just as we say that God lies in the details, greatness is often manifested in the smaller things which escape the eyes of those looking for the grandiose gesture. The reader of Kamaladevi's autobiography, *Inner Recesses, Outer Spaces*, will find that despite facing immense personal difficulties, disappointments, hostility from her peers in the handicrafts sector, and a lonely personal life, there is tremendous grace in her silence and no expression of any bitterness against others. She steers clear from the disappointments of her personal life and deliberately does not mention the antagonism and attacks from those who were part of the durbar system that was built up over the years in the Congress Party, where proximity to the Nehru family counted for more than commitment to ideals, merit and quality.

The bureaucracy had become stale and self-serving, her successors in the institutions she had worked so hard to set up had no time for her, and Faridabad had become an urban nightmare. Crafts were treated as elitist, and were losing their moorings. Yet Kamaladevi never stopped working despite witnessing a visible downslide in the values she had upheld all her life. Well into her eighties, she filed a petition in the Supreme Court of India and secured the release of minor boys who had been wrongfully jailed in Punjab through police high-handedness during the days of Sikh militancy. All the while, she continued stitching decorative borders and embroidering something new on to her handloom saris like countless rural Indian women, who work all day and yet find time to create something beautiful and ornamental for themselves. On 28 October 1988, confined to a hospital bed in Bombay, she argued that she wished to travel to Hyderabad to inaugurate a crafts exhibition. The doctors did not allow her to travel, and I was asked to step in and light the inaugural lamp in her place. It was an honour I felt unworthy of. I did it with a heavy heart, knowing that she was fighting death, which ultimately overpowered her four hours later.

In India, the imprints of truly great people remain for all time. It is the time itself that is occasionally unworthy of them. Great people are undervalued, their work undermined, and their true qualities eclipsed by the shallowness of perceptions. During occasional periods of enlightenment, their deeds shine forth with the same brightness and relevance as when they lived, worked, and led others to excel. Some of them are accorded greatness during their lifetime, while others are acknowledged and saluted only after their deaths. A third category of greats accomplish miracles in their lifetime, but suffer the agony and indignity of seeing their work slowly destroyed by people and circumstances in their twilight years. It was to this last group that Kamaladevi Chattopadhyay, the star of multiple firmaments between 1903 and 1988, believed she belonged. She said as much to me one nostalgic and reflective evening in Bangalore just a few months before her death.

Greatness brought with it the sadness of demolished dreams, and in the last months of her life she often withdrew into the sound of silence, drawing her experiences and assessments into herself. As the evening shadows darkened, she would not switch on the lamp by her side. Instead, she would speak sadly to close friends of the destruction of all that she had created around her. She took solace in the beauty of little things—music, the play of light and shadow, the leisure to dream and savour the gifts of nature. As the grand deeds of life slipped away, she realized that she was clinging to the small and very human things. It was left to those who believed in her greatness to reassure her that her work would continue in the hands of others, and nothing was lost. Others will have to judge whether these were empty assurances.

Amma: The Enigma

Sushila Ravindranath

J. Jayalalithaa's two most memorable interviews were with Simi Garewal and Karan Thapar. Simi's gushing adulation on her show, *Rendezvous with Simi Garewal*, had Jayalalithaa purring, while Thapar's deliberate needling on his version of the BBC's *Hard Talk* made her roar. But let there be no doubt—she is no kitten, but a Bengal tigress who has made the convoluted political jungles of Tamil Nadu her own territory.

In the Simi Garewal interview, Jayalalithaa relaxed enough to sing for her audience: '*Aa ja sanam, madhur chandni mein hum tum milein, to viraane mein bhi aa jayegi bahar*' ('Come, my love, let's meet on a moonlit night and this wilderness will be transformed by spring'). Simi acknowledged that 'there are a lot of people who opened up in *Rendezvous*, for example, the chief minister of Tamil Nadu, J. Jayalalithaa. Though everyone thought it would be the most difficult interview, it turned out to be one of my best.' In contrast, Karan Thapar pulled off a different sort of coup. He went for the jugular, but nearly got mauled in the process. At the end of a typically provocative interview, he tried to shake hands with the imperious lady. 'It's been great talking to you ma'am,' he offered by way of truce. She frostily refused the extended hand, choosing to respond with a regal namaste instead and retorted, 'I must say it wasn't a pleasure talking to you,' icily concluding the interview.

Somewhere between these two extremes lies the true persona of J. Jayalalithaa. No one has really fathomed her enigma or pierced her armour, or even found some clue as to what really makes her tick. She always manages to rise from adversity like the mythical phoenix, confusing her adversaries at every turn. Those closest to her—even her worst enemies—will admit that if there is one thing she doesn't lack, it is courage.

Many a foe has made the mistake of writing her political obituary several times over, but she has proved them wrong every time, smiled enigmatically, and risen from the ashes with more strength than ever before. Her enemies realize that it is a deadly mistake to underestimate her, because when she strikes back she is terrifyingly ruthless.

Love her or hate her, you cannot ignore her—this is a fact that her opponents have woefully learnt.

In the economically and culturally progressive state of Tamil Nadu, politics has been dominated by cinema for a long time, with events sometimes proving to be even more colourful than in the movies, complete with bizarre twists in the tale, larger-than-life characters and high drama. It seems fitting that it was from this world that *Puratchi Thalaivi*, the great Revolutionary Leader of the All India Anna Dravida Munnetra Kazhagam (AIADMK), J. Jayalalithaa, emerged.

Before she came to prominence as a political heavyweight, Jayalalithaa reigned as the super-heroine who could make box office registers jingle tantalizingly to her dance numbers. It was in this world that she formed her fateful association with the swashbuckling 'MGR', the late M. G. Ramachandran. It is a complex world in which reel and real merge seamlessly, more often than not into the political arena. Tamil Nadu is a state where those who rule the box office inevitably don leadership mantles, and adoring fans get easily converted into party cadres.

Over the past two decades, Tamil Nadu's destiny has been scripted by two sworn adversaries—M. Karunanidhi, the chief and patron of the Dravida Munnetra Kazhagam (DMK), and his bete noire, J. Jayalalithaa. It is between these two giants that control over the state has alternated during this time. The Tamil Nadu electorate is clear about this division. The predominantly woman-dominated rural electorate has steadfastly refused to accept that their beloved patron saint and God, the legendary MGR, is no more, and have simply transferred that blind faith and following to Amma, as Jayalalithaa is affectionately known. On the other hand, the urban and semi-urban electorate are strong DMK loyalists. The electoral math has alternately favoured both parties.

Jayalalithaa is aware that she—and she alone—has the ability to garner votes for the party. She *is* the AIADMK and without her the party is a zero, ready to be annexed or annihilated by an aggressive and rag-tag opposition. How did she acquire the political sagacity that has rendered her virtually indestructible?

Jayalalithaa was not born into a political family where ballot boxes were everyday playthings, but into a traditional Brahmin family in Mysore. Her grandfather, a government servant, got his beautiful daughter, Veda, married to the son of a doctor who was serving in the palace of the Maharaja of Mysore. Veda was barely in her teens when Jaya was born. Life was to prove treacherous for the young mother, as she soon realized that her husband was an alcoholic who had also rapidly frittered away the family fortune. Veda soon found herself a widow, with the added responsibility of looking after Jaya and her brother, Jayakumar.

Veda's sister, Vidya, was considered to be something of a rebel because she had joined the film world. The recently-widowed Veda, while on a visit to her sister in Chennai, was spotted by a producer and also got some offers. She too soon took the plunge into films, changed her name to Sandhya, and became a moderately successful film actress. Life wasn't easy, but she was determined that her children would be educated in the best schools.

And young Jaya did study in the best schools—first at the Bishop Cotton Girls' High School in Bangalore, and later at the Church Park Convent in Chennai. Her impeccable English and masterly articulation can be traced back to her years at the convent, which gave her a lasting confidence and high levels of self-esteem. She had a sophistication that not many film heroines of her time could claim to have, or even aspire to.

Jayalalithaa was an achiever in school. A star student in every respect, she was not only a topper who consistently excelled in her studies, but was also interested in sports, took part in extra-curricular activities like debating and theatre, and became a proficient dancer. When she passed out of the Church Park Convent in 1964, she was the winner of the best outgoing student award.

However, at this stage, family circumstances prevented her from studying further. She has said on many occasions that she always wanted to study further and qualify herself professionally, but life had something else in store for her. By the time she finished school, her mother had more or less stopped working in films. In any case, Sandhya had been a latecomer into the film industry, and had only got second-rung roles. The family was in dire need of money. At her mother's request, Jayalalithaa joined the film industry, debuting in director Sridhar's *Vennira Aadai* (The White

Raiment), in which she played a young widow. It must have been a harrowing sacrifice, particularly for such an excellent student. Jayalalithaa couldn't have dreamt that one day she would be not just a top heroine, but a woman of destiny in politics too.

Very few of her films can be described as 'meaningful' or categorized as 'art cinema'. They were mass entertainers, and soon producers were lining up to cash in on the box office potential of her star pairings with MGR and Sivaji Ganesan, two of the biggest cult heroes in Tamil cinema. Her first film with MGR was called *Ayirathil Oruvan* (One in a Thousand). Her expressive eyes, peaches-and-cream complexion and saucy dialogues assured her a massive fan following, but her life was in for further upheaval due to her association with MGR, who decided to take her under his wing. In the course of his movie career, they acted together in nearly thirty films. MGR came from an extremely poor background and had finally made it as a film star. Somewhere along the way he developed an interest in politics, and became a follower of C. Annadurai, the leader of the DMK.

MGR was a great vote-puller. Over the years, he had carefully cultivated his image as the screen hero who respected women, particularly the mother, sister and wife, and always stood up for the downtrodden. He never smoked or drank in his films. It was almost as if he played the same role in film after film, never doing a 'negative' role, until in the minds of the public his screen image became one with his real image. The DMK's electoral triumph in 1966, when it decisively unseated the ruling Congress Party, changed the politics of Tamil Nadu forever. C. Annadurai became the chief minister; his second-in-command, M. Karunanidhi, became a cabinet minister, while MGR continued to act in films.

Just two years after becoming chief minister, Annadurai succumbed to cancer and Karunanidhi became the chief minister. The new leader of the DMK, who had been very close to MGR during Annadurai's lifetime, now started to become wary of MGR's popularity and vote-gathering abilities. Things deteriorated to the point that MGR was compelled to leave the DMK to form his own party, which he called the All India Anna Dravida Munnetra Kazhagam, or the AIADMK, in 1972. MGR's newly-formed party won the 1977 elections decisively, winning him the chief minister's chair, which the DMK was unable to regain until after his death in 1987.

Meanwhile, at the peak of Jayalalithaa's career, her mother passed away. Her mother had handled everything, from her career to her household, and Jaya, who had until now been protected from the outside world, suddenly had to learn to deal with day-to-day problems. She had become very close to MGR, and the loss of her mother brought them even closer. She was quite open about her relationship with the late leader, calling him her 'friend, guide and philosopher'.

But it was not destined to be an easy ride. A couple of years after MGR became the chief minister of Tamil Nadu, Jayalalithaa quit films voluntarily. She was tired and bored with a career that no longer presented her with any challenges. She also had a fallout with her mentor, and it was several years before they got back together again. In these years she tried to find happiness with Shobhan Babu, a Telugu film actor, but the relationship didn't work out.

When MGR and Jayalalithaa did get back together, it was in the most dramatic way. At a typically lavish AIADMK conference he initiated her into politics, making her the propaganda secretary of the party. Like everything else she had ever chosen to do in her life, she excelled at this too, and became MGR's star pupil. As she was also known to be someone who had a mind of her own, the coterie around MGR became wary of her. MGR too, by all accounts, was not the easiest person to deal with. He is said to have been a difficult man, full of complexities, who constantly played cat-and-mouse games with her, not allowing her to relax for a moment. He made her a Rajya Sabha member, but when people in Delhi began to take notice of her and his coterie resented her, he called her back to Chennai, making it clear that she was no longer in favour. It was not a happy time for her, but she had grit, determination and staying power, and eventually survived many trials by fire to emerge as a tough politician in her own right.

In 1986, MGR fell ill and had to go to the Brooklyn Hospital in America for treatment. In his absence, Jayalalithaa effortlessly stepped into his shoes. She became the crowd-puller, and was instrumental in helping win the assembly elections in his absence, even as the knives were out for her within the party. From his hospital bed in America, MGR made her the party's general secretary amidst much heartburn and stiff opposition.

When the AIADMK won a thumping victory in that election she was seen as being anointed heir apparent, but it was not as simple as that. MGR's death in 1987 brought her great personal misery, and her party leaders lavished scorn upon her. While his body lay in state for public viewing, she stood next to it for more than twelve hours waiting to pay her respects. Short of manhandling her, her detractors could do nothing. As his body was being placed on the funeral cortege, she tried to accompany it but was pushed off by one of his widow Janaki's nephews. This humiliating moment was caught on camera. A section of the party rallied behind Janaki, and a short lived government ensued under her leadership. The party split into the Jayalalithaa and Janaki factions, creating inroads to power for the DMK for the first time in ten years.

But Janaki was not made of the same stuff as Jayalalithaa, and her government did not last long. Jayalalithaa won the elections, and now had a seat in the Tamil Nadu assembly. She then claimed that she had been roughed up by DMK leaders in the assembly, and that one of them had ripped her sari. She walked out of the assembly. In an instant, she was once again the woman the Tamil Nadu electorate loved best— the woman wronged.

All these trials and tribulations must be deeply etched in Jayalalithaa's unwavering memory, and these very memories must have kindled a fire in her to fight back and prove her mettle to the people of Tamil Nadu, not to mention her enemies. Jayalalithaa's track record as a survivor is in sharp contrast to the image she has projected to her electorate at all the significant turning points of her journey in politics. She has mastered the art of projecting herself as the injured party, the lone woman against the mighty opposition.

Jayalalithaa never relies on speechwriters and spin doctors; the ones who are part of her entourage know they are dispensable. She is capable of creating commanding speeches out of mediocre and mundane material, reads voraciously, and has a famously unerring memory which has doubtless contributed to her success, as well as fuelled her feared vindictiveness. Her fall from grace and power in 1996 in the face of rampant corruption in her cabinet, the much talked about wedding of her adopted son, and other such excesses brought the DMK back to power in the state. The DMK made the mistake of unleashing a tsunami of cases against her, even ensuring a jail stint, where she claimed cockroaches kept her company. One has to only see her lavish residence at Poes Garden in Chennai in all its opulence to understand why this jail stay made her even more determined to extract revenge.

Her party secured a sweeping victory in the 2001 state elections, no doubt helped by a massive sympathy wave where she once again came across as the woman wronged. She was the chief minister again, and wasted no time in making good the promise she had made during her campaign: 'I vow to make sure that he [Karunanidhi] eats off the same prison plate that I did.' M. Karunanidhi, her sworn enemy, was arrested in a high-voltage midnight raid, ironically, for the same charges that he had slapped against Jayalalithaa—corruption. The elderly former chief minister was dragged off to jail in his nightclothes, kicking and screaming, viewed by the entire country in now infamous television footage.

Jayalalithaa's grand comeback in 2001 was followed by her being unseated from the post of chief minister of Tamil Nadu in light of the court's verdict on the TANSI land deal case filed against her, sentencing her to three years' imprisonment. High drama followed with the installation of O. Panneerselvam as the caretaker chief minister of Tamil Nadu. 'O.P.', as he is known, was the ideal choice, someone who could be trusted as implicitly as Bharat was in the *Ramayana* when he made it explicitly clear that he was only a caretaker for the real king when he put Ram's *paduka* on the throne of Ayodhya.

Today, Jayalalithaa seems a lonely figure. She has no family to speak of. Her brother passed away a few years ago, and she does not keep up with her uncles and aunts. Her close friendship with Sasikala, whose family she has adopted, has given rise to a lot of speculation. That she went a little overboard at her foster son's wedding extravaganza, earning the dubious distinction of securing a place in the *Guinness Book of World Records* for the 'Largest Wedding Banquet', is well known. Her purported jewellery and shoe collections are reported to be extravagant enough to give Imelda Marcos a run for her money.

These excesses generated immense public resentment, and at one point no less than the superstar Rajnikanth had brought her down at the hustings with his famous quote: 'Even God cannot help Tamil Nadu if she continues in power.' Rajnikanth's superstardom and his sway over the people of the state is massive, and Jayalalithaa did not like the possibility of his looking at the chief minister's mantle, possibly even eyeing political power. But they have since kissed and made up.

Her unpredictable and changeable political alliances with various national parties have all been chronicled ad nauseam, as has her roller-coaster ride in Tamil Nadu's turbulent politics. One of the most recent examples of her extraordinary iron will was the capture of the notorious dacoit and sandalwood smuggler, Veerappan, in 2004. She had repeatedly vowed that she would get him, and the credit for exterminating the notorious 'forest brigand' lies with her inspiring leadership and her support and backing to her trusted police chief, Vijayakumar.

There has been a lot of talk about her all-pervading belief in astrology, soothsayers and religious rituals, but many feel that a person's beliefs and superstitions are his or her own. It's a very private belief system, and no one has the right to question or comment.

The conflict in Jayalalithaa's personality lies in the clash between her intellectual side and the imperious popular politician in her.

She has remained in the news for one reason or another, be it for revamping the Tamil Nadu police force, booting out non-performing ministers, announcing benevolent schemes (mainly and shrewdly targeted at women), or for firing striking government employees en masse.

More recently, Tamil Nadu's electorate predictably decided to give the DMK another chance, but few would risk writing off the lady who is now leading the largest opposition the Tamil Nadu assembly has ever seen.

Her story is still being written.

The Tapestry of Her Life

Malvika Singh

'There was a great explosion of colour, expanding and contracting; flaming reds, and the intense blue of a peacock's throat; as my sight began to return, these colours gave way to dots of grey that came together once again as tangible shapes and forms.' Pupul Jayakar had been through two weeks of complete blindness after having lost an unborn child. She had been in contact with a dog that had rabies, and the doctors had injected a full dose of anti-rabies injections; seven months pregnant, she was allergic to the drug and developed eclampsia, and with it soaring blood pressure, convulsions and total blindness. 'Blindness is not blackness,' she said. Her mind must have travelled across many levels during that period, crossing the manifold experiences of her life.

In her childhood the familiar sounds of the recitation of the *Ram Charit Manas*, the epics, and the beliefs and philosophies of India had come down to her through the spoken word, the oral tradition—a tradition by which India communicated with past generations.

Her father was a liberal intellectual in the civil service, driven by the passion of that generation to participate and determine change and growth. Her mother came from a Gujarati Brahmin family, and was rooted in its strong cultural traditions. The security of these two strands, their diversity and yet their common values, are what must have been the greatest influence on her. Clearly, it is what gave her a base to build upon.

She recalled having spent weeks travelling as part of her father's entourage through the districts, camping in villages, sometimes in wide-open spaces, often amidst mango groves. A camp meant a mobile home with all the familiar paraphernalia. Through this exposure she never felt unrooted. She began to absorb the nuances of India, its contradictions, disparities and congenital strengths. Early years are always the most impressionable, and often establish the ethics and values of one's future.

Fakirs and itinerant storytellers would collect at the camp on their nomadic routes, sharing what they had to say, telling their ancient tales. Bards would sing and recite verses that encompassed the history and way of life of the region. This bottomless archive is what Pupul began to delve into from a very early age, and this is what she continued to draw on in the future to disseminate and interpret. She had always given precedence to 'feeling' and 'seeing' the textures of a civilization. When asked by Jawaharlal Nehru to help set up the handloom industry after Independence, Pupul launched what in many ways was a revolution in the world of fabric and clothing in India. She encapsulated her range of experience into one specific area and successfully established the HHEC (Handloom and Handicraft Export Corporation), which put traditional Indian skills on the world map. Her experiences of life manifested into something tangible, which could regenerate and nurture an inherent need for a tested tradition. That is, in fact, the definition of true culture.

From the life of a civil servant's child, she was plunged

once a year into the ambience of a traditional Brahmin home in Surat. She was therefore never free from the authenticity of India. The influence of her father was strong and he instilled in Pupul an interest in reading and meeting all manner of people ranging from pundits to philosophers.

At the age of eleven she went to Benares, to a school started by Annie Besant, the great Theosophist active in India's freedom movement. Here, she began to get rooted more confidently in the true life and ambience of India. The many images and myriad passing encounters from her childhood began to crystallize. Early mornings were spent walking with her father, strolling under clusters of cork trees, talking endlessly about everything. She shed western dress and took to wearing saris. It was only while riding that she wore breeches!

Her father was posted to Allahabad when she was fifteen. It was there that she met Jawaharlal Nehru and his family. To her, as to many others of her generation, Panditji was a great source of inspiration, a symbol of the future and of their lives.

When she was eighteen, Pupul left for England to train as a journalist, and it was there that she met Jackie, the man she married. In 1937 she became Pupul Jayakar and settled with her husband in Bombay. Radhika, her first child, was born in 1938. In 1939 she became pregnant again. That child she lost along with her sight. She was shattered. Worse still, as she began to come to terms with her personal trauma, she lost her father, whom she had been excessively close to. He had been a firm influence and stable anchor in her life. The year was 1940.

Another phase of Pupul Jayakar's life was about to begin. For the decade that followed, she involved herself in political activity. She worked with Mridula Sarabhai as her assistant in the Kasturba Trust and was also assistant secretary of women's affairs in the National Planning Committee. In the course of those years she met Gandhiji twice, went to Sevagram and was exposed to Gandhian attitudes, but was never deeply moved by Gandhi. She admired him for the 'precision of his mind, his understanding of the nuts and bolts of development'. In 1942, the Quit India movement took her to the forefront of the agitation for freedom, but a sudden attack of appendicitis followed by surgery kept her away from any active participation.

In 1945, Pupul Jayakar had a third baby. Born deformed, the infant died within three weeks. This was another link in a chain of emotional upheavals and personal tragedy. That same year, Jawaharlal Nehru was released from British custody in prison. He encouraged Pupul to get involved in the co-operative and development movements, which she did. For a while during that phase of her life, Pupul became interested in the Socialist Party. In 1947, both the Congress and the Socialist parties offered her a seat to contest the elections. She declined and moved away from politics. It was possibly that decision which led her on to the most important and substantial decade of her working life.

During this time Pupul met Jiddu Krishnamurti. She had accompanied her mother on a visit, and vividly recalls the initial encounter. In her words, 'This figure was immensely beautiful. There was a silence in him that you could touch and feel.' In the course of that first conversation, Krishnamurti asked her why she worked. She left feeling a trifle angry, but was drawn to the tremendous sense of truth that Krishnaji radiated.

Through those years, Pupul had been at the centre of the social whirl of Bombay. Then, quite out of the blue, she began to feel like an outsider, an alien within the society set.

That life seemed to be out of sync with her true being. She went back to Krishnaji and thereon began a long-standing relationship of much speaking and discussion, a sharing of ideas.

'He was a great listener. Then, one day I had a message that he wanted to see me. His listening had ended. Hearing him, the artificial dam cracked open and a river of scars and sorrows burst forth. My life and perceptions began to change. I began to go within myself, to grapple with the despair and darkness, to begin to come to terms with myself. For this I realized one needed no guru, no anchor except the disciplined quest to know oneself. Man is caught in opposites which have to conflict. Perception is action—if perception is true. I work, and through that experience I have discovered one great truth—not to carry over anything; to work in the today. The energy that is released brings with it insight and the creative channels of the mind open. Perception is a state of total attention. The immobility of the mind creates and it goes on to generate an energy that sustains. The brain doesn't necessarily age as one grows old.'

From 1950 onwards, Pupul Jayakar worked towards moulding her ideas and beliefs into reality. When Jawaharlal Nehru and T.R. Krishnamachari asked her to take a look at the handloom sector and launch a viable industry, she extricated herself from evenings of poker and bridge at the Willingdon Club in Bombay and set out to teach herself what the business of textiles was all about. As she herself once explained, 'A piece of fabric is a synthesis of texture, colour and design.' Her inherent, instinctive response to all three was latent, and she now consciously began to follow her judgement through by studying the complex subject in practical and real terms.

She was fortunate to have had what many do not—tacit, unflinching support. This she used to build service centres, marketing structures and institutions for the weavers. The support enabled her to create the tangible and taught her what she considered a prime lesson: 'When you see or spot true talent, give it your total support and it will never let you down. I hope I have been able to do likewise with many young people.' In the sphere of handlooms she says with disarming honesty and pride, 'My living heritage is manifested in Mapu. [Mapu being Martand Singh.] He is carrying forward what I was able to initiate. I found him, backed him, made him go out there into the field and see for himself, experience, learn and then develop.' About Rajeev Sethi she said, 'He has an ancient mind in a young body.' These were her two primary proteges.

With her involvement in the regeneration of India's second-largest economic sector after agriculture, she brought about, possibly inadvertently, a radical change in the dress and style of the urban woman in India. To wear handloom saris became fashionable for the chiffon-clad elite. The more traditional, the better. Today, compared to the average urban man, the Indian woman is undoubtedly better dressed. Yes, this is a value judgement, but often such judgements do trigger off a trend, a movement that helps nurture an indigenous attitude within an environmental need.

By inviting the French designer Pierre Cardin to India when she was heading the Handicrafts and Handlooms Export Corporation of the Government of India, she put Indian textiles on the international map. He worked with Indian fabrics and designed a new collection. Thereafter, many leading fashion designers from Europe and America delved into the trove of Indian textiles, using them for creations of high fashion. Fabrics from India made an impact on the world market. Today, this may appear to be the most obvious thing to have done, but at the time it was a calculated risk. And the risk worked. A risk that indirectly set the stage for establishing institutions of design and fashion in India. She remained involved in both.

Pupul Jayakar never shied away from taking risks. Rather, such risks of entering unknown areas and markets seemed to spur on an increased energy and spirit in her. With every unconventional idea and decision that she initiated, Pupul was besieged by vast doses of criticism and sometimes abuse. Instead of collapsing under this or retracting from her position, she came into her own, taking on the challenge and refusing to crumble under pressure.

She was, more often than not, accused of operating with the assistance of a small, handpicked coterie of people. Her explanation, when confronted, was that she did not believe in building and creating large, cumbersome infrastructures and institutions. She always found it easier and more effective to work with smaller groups. In actual terms though, doing what she did in the handloom sector, Pupul involved and supported huge numbers of people in specialized areas of work.

Indira Gandhi had asked her to initiate the Festival of India abroad in an effort to enhance India's great tradition of craft skills and culture. When a tirade against these festivals began to gain ground, Pupul's reaction was characteristic. At a press conference in early 1985, where she was questioned about not having spoken with the press earlier she said, 'The country has recently gone through the worst trauma of many decades and at many different levels. Those realities surely take priority and precedence over our festivals abroad. Now, since we are about to inaugurate one in France and another in the United States, I am confident that the events as they unfold will bring in the bouquets. We hope these festivals will reveal the great strengths of a young nation with an ancient culture and heritage.'

Pupul Jayakar also set up the Indian National Trust for Art and Cultural Heritage (INTACH). It was something that Indira Gandhi wanted done and she in her personal capacity, along with Pupul, formed the trust and had it registered. Founder members were invited to join and thereafter, membership was thrown open. Through the first decade, INTACH struggled to find a space for itself. It identified architects, researchers, volunteers who believed in restoration and conservation of India's multi-layered heritage. Over the years, INTACH took on conservation studies and projects, and gradually established itself across India.

Volunteers in scores of cities and towns came together to create the many chapters of this organization. It was a huge task, a very challenging one, and it worked. It began to change the mindset towards this critical space that was till then controlled and determined by the Archaeological Survey of India. Today, conservation is an intrinsic part of every discussion and debate in the realm of planning and development. But having set the ground, the trust itself has grown 'old'. The ethos she had infused into it is no longer there. The young, fresh, creative and passionate minds are outside of INTACH. The trust has been taken over by retired administrators instead of another generation of men and women looking towards the future. Its soul has been replaced. That is the difference between the likes of Pupul and her times, and those at the helm today.

What was pioneering in her persona was the ability to take the plunge, to always accept a challenge, to never be deterred by the impossible. The young band of people who worked with her believed in her and worked with a passion. They were of another generation, and saw a future in what they were doing. She was a mentor. She never competed with her proteges, but groomed them. She too kept pace with a changing world through her young colleagues, and was never condescending towards them. Age was never a barrier with her, and respect for those with a spark was always forthcoming.

This striving to discover herself in relation to her work, colleagues and environment, her ability to see her own weaknesses and strengths, her acceptance of criticism without the accompanying arrogance, her childlike quality of accepting a wrong when pointed out—all came together to make her what she was. Very complex, but utterly straightforward and forthright. These personal traits and her constantly growing fund of knowledge gave her supreme confidence in herself.

'The brain does not age,' she said, and she was right. Hers was sharper and younger than most.

Upping the Ante

Naazneen Karmali

9–18 March and 7 April 2004. After consulting the Hindu calendar, these were the dates that Yamini Mazumdar pronounced 'auspicious'. Trusting her mother's instinct in such matters, Kiran Mazumdar declared to her bankers that Biocon, her pioneering biotech venture, would open its public issue on 9 March 2004, and list on the stock exchange on 7 April. Kiran's bankers, veterans like Hemendra Kothari of DSP Merrill-Lynch and Naina Lal Kidwai of HSBC, knew better than to argue against such 'illogic'. When the businesswoman in Kiran Mazumdar made up her mind, it was best to consider it a 'done deal' and go along with it.

The bankers' misgivings, which they surely must have harboured and expressed, were not unfounded. On the face of it, Biocon's first ever public issue seemed on a suicidal course, timed smack in the middle of a spate of big-ticket equity issues. It was not just ordinary companies that Biocon would be up against, but public sector giants like ONGC, which were entering the stock market at the same time. But Kiran's trust in her mother's instincts paid off, and Biocon's public issue was oversubscribed.

It takes a certain kind of self-confidence and bravado for a Rs 500 crore biotech company, whose business model ordinary folk can barely understand, to compete for investors' money alongside a government-owned and backed behemoth.

All the tipping points in Kiran Mazumdar's eventful life have come about this way—propelled by her ability to shut out the cacophony created by naysayers, Kiran has an uncanny knack of being able to listen to her inner voice and seize the moment. And what a glorious moment it was that April morning when her company's shares were to be listed on the National Stock Exchange in Mumbai. As she pressed the button and the ticker came to life, Biocon's shares began trading. The company's market capitalization skyrocketed to $1 billion and, as the largest shareholder, Kiran became India's richest woman in a matter of minutes.

Although her stock market debut made her an instant crorepati, she is no overnight sensation. She has built Biocon brick-by-brick with spunk, perseverance and plain old hard work. Kiran had no business background when she started out—her father was a professional brewmaster—nor did she have a management degree; yet Biocon is among the top twenty biotech companies in the world today, and still aiming higher. Kiran is a rare person—a self-made woman entrepreneur in a country where women tend to get into business mainly through family connections.

Kiran's success story represents a paradigm shift in entrepreneurship in India over the last couple of decades. There was a time when you had to be rich to get richer. Since the 1980s, a new breed of entrepreneur has emerged, men and women who have no inheritances or family connections in business. These self-made entrepreneurs have built companies by leveraging intellectual capital and created 'knowledge businesses'. Like N.R. Narayana Murthy of Infosys and Azim Premji of Wipro, Kiran is embarrassed to be labelled 'rich'. Her real contribution, her raison d'etre, she maintains, is creating intellectual wealth, and building a world-class bio-pharma company from India.

Kiran had a lot going against her when she started out. She was a woman, and at only twenty-five, a young one at that. Her chosen field was biotechnology, an area nobody really knew very much about at the time. Somehow, Kiran turned these negatives to her advantage. Few people really understood Biocon's business model, even though they may have known Kiran or known of her. Although Biocon started out as a maker of industrial enzymes, over time she cleverly positioned it to move into bio-pharmaceuticals, where she saw her future. It was this leap that changed the stakes for Kiran and Biocon.

Nothing in Kiran Mazumdar's background could have suggested that she would go on to scale such heights in the corporate world. She was born into an upper-middle class Gujarati family in Bangalore. The Mazumdars (originally 'Majmudars', or revenue collectors) hailed from Baroda, but Kiran's father's job as a brewmaster took him to Bangalore. Employed with the Mallya-owned United Breweries group, R.I. Mazumdar was India's first brewmaster. He had studied brewing at Edinburgh and was urbane, polished and had impeccably refined tastes—qualities that Kiran, the eldest of three children (and the only daughter), imbibed. Growing up, Kiran was closest to her father, with whom she shared a special bond. She confesses that in school she was a bit ashamed of her father's work, as the liquor business was looked down upon in those days.

Ironically, Kiran got into business quite by accident. Originally, she wanted to be a doctor, but didn't get into medical college. Although she got the marks to qualify, she flunked the pre-admission interview when she confessed that

she couldn't stand the sight of blood! Kiran begged her father
to pay the capitation fees to procure a seat, but her principled
father would have none of it—either she got in on merit, or
not at all. Looking back at that angst-ridden time, Kiran
admits that it was a wise decision, as she would probably
not have been a very good doctor.

After completing her bachelor's degree in zoology from
Bangalore University, Kiran decided to take up her father's
profession and flew to Australia to study malting and
brewing. An excellent student, she scored a first class at both
the graduate and post-graduate levels. When she came back
to India in 1975, a freshly qualified brewmaster from
Australia, Kiran was all set to follow in her father's footsteps.
But the brewing business in India was extremely male-
dominated, and the best job she could get was in quality
assurance and not operations, where the real action lay. Even
Vittal Mallya, her father's employer, discouraged her saying,
'It is very tough for us to accept you as a brewmaster.'

After scouting around for jobs in several places, Kiran
managed to land a job at a company called Moray Firth
Maltings in Scotland as an assistant brewer. She began
preparations to leave for Inverness, and would in all likelihood
have been just another statistic in the brain drain out of India.
At that time, she recalls, being a brewmaster was her ultimate
ambition. But fate unexpectedly came calling in the form of
Les Auchincloss, the founder of a small biotech start-up in
Ireland. He had been referred to Kiran by one of her professors
in Melbourne, and was visiting India. Would she be interested
in helping him market and manufacture industrial enzymes
in India? Biocon Ireland was a buyer of papaine, extracted
from papaya, which grows abundantly in India. It also bought

isin glass, a protein extracted from the swim bladders of tropical fish.

Intrigued, Kiran unpacked her bags and stayed back. It was a major gamble for her, as in those days most educated Indians were highly enamoured of the West, and were keen to work abroad. But taking risks has always been a hallmark of Kiran's career. In 1978, Biocon was formed with Rs 1 lakh as seed capital; a 70:30 venture between Biocon Ireland and Kiran. It was a low-tech operation at first, and its first 'factory' was in reality nothing more than a small garage in Bangalore.

Kiran had a tough time convincing banks to give her loans, with bankers insisting that she get her father to guarantee the loans, something she stoutly refused to do. Finding people who wanted to work for her was another challenge. The interviewees who showed up almost always mistook her for the secretary, not the boss! Very few people were willing to bet their careers on her fledgling venture— now, of course, it's a different story and Biocon is flooded with resumes not just from India, but all over the world.

Somehow, Kiran managed to assemble a team of likeminded professionals around her, who stayed on at Biocon. The head of the R&D department, Shrikumar Suryanarayan, joined straight out of IIT. The chief of operations, Arun Chandavarkar, had the pick of the best jobs as an MIT graduate, but opted for the challenge of working with Biocon. Marketing frontman Ajay Bhardwaj and chief financial officer Murali Krishnan joined from bigger companies. Kiran's home-grown management style, which is very hands-on, has kept this senior team together. There is an air of easy informality in their interactions, and an amazing lack of hierarchical barriers between people.

Thinking big has been another Kiran trademark. In 1984,

Kiran decided that her modest business model was not exciting enough, and the real challenge lay in becoming a full-scale biotech company. After convincing her Irish partners that they were up to the job, Biocon extended its range of products, moving into speciality foods, and bakery and textile enzymes. But another twist of fate awaited Kiran. In 1988, Biocon Ireland was sold to the Anglo-Dutch giant Unilever, and Kiran now found herself with a powerful new partner.

But Kiran has always had a great sense of curiosity, and an immense capacity to learn. She picked up the best from her multinational partner—HRD, systems and corporate governance practices—and used this time as an opportunity to improve her own company, and gained an entry point into international markets. Biocon had a global outlook right from the start, as most of its customers were overseas. Quality was of ultimate importance, and Kiran developed a fetish for it. Even today, she is unwilling to compromise on this in any way and is committed to providing world-class quality for everything she does.

When Unilever decided to sell its chemicals business to ICI, Kiran faced the prospect of finding herself in bed with yet another partner. By then she had imbibed everything she needed to from Unilever and realized one thing—if she wanted to grow, she would have to cut the apron strings. For by then, Kiran had decided that Biocon's future would be infinitely more exciting if she went beyond enzymes and got into the big-stakes world of bio-pharmaceuticals.

Since Unilever wasn't interested in pharma, Kiran exercised her preemptive rights to buy over Unilever's stake in Biocon. By then she had married the Scotsman John Shaw, a multinational executive who was posted to Bangalore as the head of Coates Viyella's Indian subsidiary. John used his savings to invest in Biocon and moved to Bangalore—his life's best investment, he readily admits. It was after this that Biocon really took off. The company moved into the world of generic drugs, focusing on cholesterol-reducing drugs known as statins. Statins are blockbuster drugs that are now considered 'magic bullets'.

Along the way came a chance meeting with some scientists from the Swedish company AstraZeneca, which took Kiran into contract research. In 1994, she set up a subsidiary company called Syngene, which undertook research and development work for big pharma companies that wanted to outsource to save both time and costs in drug development. Subsequently, she also got into 'development'—doing clinical trials through another subsidiary, Clinigene. With these two subsidiaries, Biocon had all the pieces in place to blossom into a fully integrated bio-pharma company. Today, it is involved in manufacturing, drug discovery, undertaking clinical trials and marketing drugs.

Rather than making cheap knock-offs, Kiran's focus has always been on products that have a high technological or regulatory barrier. That way she can get premium prices for her products and services, as well as fulfil her aspiration of becoming a research-driven new age drug company. When Biocon launched Insugen, the brand of recombinant human insulin developed by it using a proprietary Pichia expression system, it was quite a feat. It is extremely difficult to make r-human insulin, and the market is dominated by less than a handful of multinationals. In anticipation of Biocon's launch, foreign companies cut their own insulin prices.

Biocon's next big project is a joint venture with a Cuban research institute to develop drugs for head and neck cancers. Kiran dreams that Biocon will one day discover its own drugs to cure intractable illnesses. Although her company's market value is over $1 billion, Kiran wants Biocon to be a $1 billion company not just in market capitalization but in sales. Biocon is in the throes of a Rs 700 crore expansion in Bangalore to make that dream into a reality.

Despite her all-consuming involvement with Biocon, Kiran has numerous other interests. She is the flag bearer of the Indian biotech industry, and takes that role very seriously. She is a major figure on the conference circuit, where she holds forth on India's biotech potential. She's helped set up ABLE (Association for Biotech Led Enterprises), the biotech industry's own association. She has also been the driving force behind the Institute for Biotech and Bioinformatics (IBAB).

As the chairperson and mission leader of the CII's National Task Force on Biotechnology, she has led several delegations to the USA, Canada and the UK to propel India into the global super-league of biotech trailblazers. She chairs Karnataka's Vision Group on Biotechnology, and also serves on the Board of Science Foundation, Ireland. Awards have been plentiful, but the most cherished is the Padma Shri which she was awarded in 1989 and the Padma Bhushan she was awarded more recently.

Kiran is media-savvy, and has been written about by a host of international publications—journalists from *Time*, *Newsweek*, the *New York Times* and *Forbes* have all come away impressed after meeting her. Biocon is her passion, her baby, and even today she works with all the passion of a start-up entrepreneur. Long before Biocon entered the public domain, Kiran ensured that the best practices of corporate governance were followed in her company. Her board has distinguished international names like Neville Bain, the former deputy CEO of Cadbury Schweppes, and MIT professor of chemical & biochemical engineering, Charles Cooney. In addition, Biocon has a scientific advisory board packed with luminaries like C.N.R. Rao, Sam Pasternack, Ashok Ganguly and Bala Manian. Long before stock options became prevalent in the Indian knowledge industry, Kiran introduced them in Biocon, ensuring the loyalty of her top executives who are now, thanks to the public issue, crorepatis in their own right.

Despite her phenomenal success, Kiran remains very down to earth. Her Jaeger business suits with her trademark scarf are nothing new. That Western-style dress code is something she sported even as a struggling entrepreneur. Ask her friends what success has done to Kiran and they will retort, 'Nothing. She's the same old Kiran!'—plain-speaking to the point of being blunt; someone with a great capacity for fun. Even today, despite the pressures of a multitude of commitments, Kiran still finds time to carefully plan out April Fool's jokes on her close friends: during Biocon's IPO, she sent out fake share allotment letters to her pals.

Her paper wealth has not altered her lifestyle in any major way. Although Biocon prides itself on being the Infosys of the biotech world, Kiran makes no pretensions of being another N.R. Narayana Murthy, who is almost Gandhian in his personal habits. She likes the good life, and lives in style. Yet, she is not likely to go to the extremities of good living either. Owning a private jet, for example, is more for the likes of her childhood pal Vijay Mallya. For India's richest woman, life is not a party. She works harder than ever and travels constantly around the globe. There is no letting up.

Some years ago, she and her husband John moved from the tony Koramangala area in Bangalore into Glenmore, a sprawling Spanish-style villa close to Biocon's factory. The couple frequently entertain friends and business associates there, and often host company bashes and conclaves as well. This airy, open house, where every wall is filled with art, reflects their personalities. Although it is exceedingly well-appointed, there is nothing garish or ostentatious about it. Every aspect of it was planned by them together, from the 'cave' that houses John's prized collection of wines to the adjoining guesthouse where so many of their friends have partaken of their generous hospitality.

Both Glenmore and its owners have an aura about them. But if you look closer, you will see them for what they are. Glenmore, despite the luxurious accoutrements, is home. Kiran is a woman on a mission called Biocon, still as driven as she was when she started her business from a garage twenty-seven years ago.

The Miracle Mother

Reeta Devi

I was sixteen years old when I first met Mother Teresa. I was a difficult and rather headstrong young woman; a handful for my mother to control. She was having problems with me, and in desperation mentioned her concerns to Dr B.C. Roy, the then chief minister of West Bengal. He was a man for whom I had enormous respect and he was, in many ways, my role model and hero. He had great admiration and respect for Mother Teresa, and was a great support to her in those early years. To him, Mother Teresa was 'that European nun who visits me every morning when I am attending to my patients and passes me a slip of paper with a request, asking for something for the poor.' In the early sixties, B.C. Roy persuaded my mother to introduce me to Mother. I never looked back. Mother changed my life, and gave it strength and purpose.

She moved away from her nun's robes and starched head scarves, donning a sari which gently draped her fragile frame, using its *anchal* to cover her head. This single gesture made her stand apart as an 'Indian' nun, having created an indigenous 'uniform' for her Sisters of Charity. When I met her she held both my hands in hers in a joint namaste, smiling with warmth, her eyes twinkling with laughter, exuding happiness and compassion. I was drawn to her from that moment on. I began to work with her in Calcutta and assist the other nuns, who were the exact opposite of those in habit I was familiar with—prissy, prim and proper. These women were brimming with fun, constantly giving of themselves.

My interaction with Mother was minimal. But when she was among us there was laughter—lots of laughter—she gave it a great deal of importance. She wanted to see smiling faces regardless of the people's plight. She believed that being happy was the start of a cure. Being young and in some ways carefree, I would spend my time clowning around with the children in Mother's home, enjoying every moment with them and the nuns. Life continued on an even keel.

When the Pope came to India he gave Mother the bullet-proof Cadillac that he had brought along with him. As she had no use for such a car, she decided to auction it and raise some money. Each ticket for the lottery was priced at a hundred rupees. Bhim, my husband, discovered that the actor Shammi Kapoor had bought ten thousand rupees worth of tickets. I naively mentioned this fact to Mother. Horrified, she stopped the lottery, forced a visiting old Parsi gentleman to buy one ticket and handed the car over to him, saying that Jesus had intervened. No lotteries ever thereafter! This is how she dealt with problems of greed for material things at all costs, of always wanting more.

In 1967 many women from wealthy, boxwallah backgrounds worked for Mother Teresa. They spent time distributing clothes, raising money and caring for the sick and destitute, bonding with each other, drawn to Mother's home, but it was never to boost their egos or feel they had to rid themselves of any sense of guilt. Mother never encouraged that. They were there because they were drawn to the remarkable and very special persona of Mother. No questions asked, they did her bidding.

One day, just before Christmas, one of these women rang me and asked if I could take some collections to Nirmal Hriday, a home for the dying in Kalighat. She had her children home from boarding school and could not go herself. I had never been there before, and she warned me that it would be grim, that I should prepare myself to face the situation. I mustered up as much courage as I could and decided to go. When I finally walked into Nirmal Hriday, I felt I had entered a peaceful abode. It was a calm, strangely happy environment.

The nuns welcomed me. They were all smiling, and had time for everyone. Around me were hundreds of destitute people who Mother would pick up off the roads. They were suffering, but seemed at peace here. Something inexplicable happened to me there. I connected instantly with Nirmal Hriday and made it mine as well. There was no regimen to my days there. I worked when I wanted, and for as long as I wanted. I began to spend a lot of time there and, on Sundays, when my husband Bhim was out playing golf or at the races, I would go to Kalighat, scrub the floors and fight with Mother to allow me to clean the toilets (something she always wanted to do herself). Finally, one Sunday, the nuns cautioned me to 'allow' Mother to clean the toilets, since it was her offering to Jesus on the day of the Sabbath. I backed off, not wanting to be the cause of any tension between Jesus and Mother!

In those days I was a congenital gambler, often betting at the Calcutta races. The race course was my temple. Mother knew of my weakness and ignored it. I would win lots of money, and the deal was that the cash would go towards the celebration of Christmas at the home. Some of it was sent to other such centres for the same purpose, as well as for gifts for the children and other inmates. Since we were always broke, these winnings helped us to tide over such occasions. Bhim and I were also great party animals then, and would be out till the wee hours of the morning. Invariably, it would be an effort to make it to morning mass and lunch on Christmas day. One year Mother found me dozing off on my knees, and next Christmas the timings were pushed back for us! That was how considerate, accommodating and surprising she could be.

Another year on Christmas, while we were praying in silence, there was a loud clanging sound. We turned to see where it came from, and found an inmate who had come to Nirmal Hriday from jail, his shackles still around him, making his way to the *jalebis* that I had brought for lunch. We looked to Mother to see how she would react, based on which we too would react. In her deep and resonant voice she simply said, 'Let him be'. He was immediately christened '*jalebi chor*'. She was tolerant, accepting of others' needs, aspirations and weaknesses, and would always try to make people understand how such attributes could be used to help bring happiness to others. It was an important lesson for me.

She had no hard and fast rules. She did not impose any dos and don'ts—there were no commandments. I recall having a coughing fit in Mother's presence, which was a direct result of smoking too much. I was a chain-smoker and Mother chided me gently, saying that I was smoking too much. A month later I had given up smoking and proudly announced my feat to Mother, who held my hands, looked into my eyes with the usual perceptiveness and said, 'I did not tell you to stop smoking; I said you smoke too much.' Moderation was another trait that Mother instilled in me.

Kalighat was my first love, and it was becoming my life.

That is where I bonded with people, where I learned that laughter and happiness go together with humility, and that all people, regardless of their condition, completely identify with these two sentiments. Mother taught me about love. She taught me how to give, expecting nothing in return. She taught me that love means doing unconditionally for others. She taught me that to give love unconditionally makes one happy with themselves, making it possible to give more and more.

Mother was terribly broadminded, but she would always make it a point to ask me whether I had accompanied Bhim to a party or not, what time he came home, whether he ventured out on his own, emphasizing that we should always go out together. But another time when there were some adverse, taunting comments about a widow who had become pregnant, her retort was blunt and matter of fact. 'Why? She is a widow and she is like any other woman.'

It put an end to the derision.

Her sense of humour was unmatched. Once, while visiting a minister in government in the 1980s, she talked about the wide variety of people from all professions that came to Kalighat and other homes of a similar kind that she had set up. His comment was, 'Yes Mother, it must be like the United Nations.' Mother was quick in her response: 'No, not at all, there they talk, here we work.'

By this point in my life, short of being a Missionary of Charity, a nun, I was like everyone else at the home. We built our first night shelter at Sealdah, where we were squatters on government land. The plot was at a dead end near the railway station, and it was here that we wanted to construct the building. It was to be a night shelter and day school where people would make coir products like mats and other everyday things out of waste coconut fibre.

A wealthy friend from the tea business took charge of the project and had the shelter built. In those days business people would donate silently and unconditionally, without publicizing their commitment. We managed to complete the building, but there was a hitch—it was not legal under the municipal laws. Once again, Mother found a solution. She invited Ranjit Gupta, the local police chief, to be the guest of honour for the inauguration. In her welcome speech Mother said, 'This is God's land. It was lying over here waiting to be shared with other people. I hope Ranjit Gupta will allow us to stay here.' Needless to say, Gupta legalized the land and the building.

Mother Teresa was the most focused woman I have ever met. Her love for human beings went beyond the call of 'religion'. Religion was her personal faith. She believed in Jesus and walked the earth with her hand in his. Her miracles are the missions she has nurtured, from Chernobyl to Australia, from South America to India—wherever she could—with her Missionaries of Charity. She linked the poor to love and happiness, to dignity in life, despite the anguish and the squalor that surrounded them. As always, there were initial problems. I remember the time when the nuns decided to set up shelters in Bihar. Two of them had to be closed down due to societal and administrative difficulties. The sisters were worried about living in remote areas; that the flimsy bars on the windows of the home would provide no protection. They were worried about being assaulted. Mother intervened laughingly: 'Do not worry. You all are so ugly, only Jesus can love you!' She always tried to simplify the lives of people and sort out their problems, and she always did so with lightness and a sense of humour.

In 1976, Bhim and I left India and moved to Dubai for

some years, as Bhim had a job there. Mother wrote to us in longhand with reams of news about Calcutta, about our friends, about the nuns, keeping us connected. She made us feel very special. When we returned in 1980, Nirmal Hriday had been relocated to Majnu ka Tila, on a piece of land that had been allocated to Mother by Indira Gandhi. Her son Sanjay Gandhi had been very supportive and had sent the 'Sanjay Brigade' to help clear the land. He had promised to help the sisters with whatever else they required during those early days in Delhi. Sister Margaret Mary, one of the first to join the order, was in Delhi to inaugurate the home. One afternoon, while we were reminiscing about the Calcutta days, she reminded me about how broke they used to be and how the nuns would sit in front of empty *thalis*, imagining that there was dal and rice and vegetables in front of them to eat! They would say grace and thank the Lord for what they had, get up and move away. It was yet another example of positive thinking and Mother's amazing ability to conquer the negative aspects of a situation.

Conversion took on a completely different definition with Mother. She converted people to another way of life, to love and unconditional giving. That was what she preached, by word and by action. Once, en route to the hospice we had set up in Guwahati, we were travelling with some Salesian priests who suggested to Mother that I, a Hindu, 'embrace Jesus' and be baptized. 'She could be baptized tomorrow morning—wouldn't it be a wonderful gift for Jesus?' I was horrified. I thought to myself, my god, I can't even be a good Hindu, how on earth am I going to be a good Christian? I couldn't imagine myself going to mass at 5 a.m. and going to confessional.

Mother tried to change the subject several times, but the

priests persisted. When we finally arrived at the home, Mother sent for me. I was delighted, assuming she was going to praise me and appreciate the fact that this institution, which I had personally been in charge of setting up, was one of the first AIDS hospices for the abject poor in the area. I had fought many odds to establish the home, and was expecting a pat on the back. Instead, she held my hand and said very gently, 'Reeta, do you know Jesus? He loves you as you are. Stay as you are.' Perhaps she sensed my discomfort, and never asked me to embrace Christianity.

The Mother Teresa whom I was fortunate to know was normal and human, with neither hype nor any stilted formality. We could relax and gossip and laugh with her like we could with our other friends. This openness drew many people towards her, some of whom used her good offices for their own personal ends. One such person who latched on to her even tried to get a petrol pump allocated on her behalf! Mother had gone to visit Sonia Gandhi. She was looking at some papers, and turned to Mother and asked if she really wanted a petrol pump. Mother was horrified, and made it perfectly clear that no, she certainly did not want a petrol pump, for what would she do with it?

She later confronted the man, who said he needed an income to keep his family going as he was doing voluntary work for her. Mother's response was predictable: 'I did not ask you to work here. Your first duty is to your family. That is how you serve God.'

In 1989 I lost a friend to AIDS. The death affected me in a very fundamental way, and I became obsessed by the virtually insurmountable problem of this illness. I had seen a clip in a documentary in which a patient had been treated in an inhuman manner, shackled and sent to jail, where he died like a pariah animal. I resolved to set up a hospice that would allow the poorest of the poor to die in dignity. I chose Guwahati as the location, and after going back and forth over many meetings with the administration there, Hiteshwar Saikia (the then chief minister) released some land for the project. I wanted Mother and the Sisters of Charity to run the hospice, but Mother refused. I was devastated and tried to persuade the other Sisters to convince her. One day I was summoned to go and meet her. A trifle nervous, I ventured into her room, which was her private space. She began by asking me where Bhim was. When I said that my husband was in Delhi, she asked how long I had been away from him. I told her I had been in Assam fighting for the land, and had not been home for two months. She was horrified and retorted by saying, 'This is what I do not like about you Reeta, your first duty is to Bhim. Charity begins at home.'

Mother was enigmatic, and never judgemental. She symbolized hope and brought joy and a sense of security to all those who came into her circle. Mother and her endeavours went beyond the call of religion and faith. She was 'Ma Teresa' to Kali *bhakts*, and transcended all faiths. She believed in the power of prayer, and most importantly, she had conquered her ego and dissolved into a sea of love and giving.

That is the lesson Mother has left for us mortals.

A Rich Canvas

Nitin Bhayana

With each passing decade, the legend of Amrita Sher-Gil continues to grow. Amrita could justifiably be called one of India's foremost modern painters, as her work transcended the traditional, classical artistic practices prevailing in India at the time. She was able to take Indian art, which had undergone the excesses of the illustrative Bengal school aesthetic, into a new realm. Being part-Indian, part-European, her work effortlessly blended western portraiture with an Indian ethos that made it special and unusual, and changed the way we look at contemporary art in India.

It is not for these reasons alone that the Sher-Gil legend continues to intensify. Her free spirit, a bohemian yet aristocratic style of life within a bourgeoisie background, a Parisian education, passionate sexual encounters with both men and women and, finally, her untimely death shrouded in mystery, have all contributed to making her beauty and her work virtually immortal. Even though she only lived till the age of twenty-eight, her life encompassed extraordinary experiences, and the kind of trials and tribulations that legends are made of.

Amrita painted a small number of paintings in her brief career. Of these, only a few can be said to be fully 'resolved', or in fact successful, but these are some of the most seminal works of Indian art in the twentieth century.

Amrita was born on 30 January 1913 in Budapest, Hungary. Her mother, Marie Antoinette Gottesmann, had come to visit India on the invitation of her friend, Princess Bamba, the granddaughter of Maharaja Ranjit Singh. It was during this trip to Simla in 1911 that she met her future husband, the aristocratic Umrao Singh Sher-Gil, who came from a wealthy, landowning feudal family in Punjab. Umrao Singh's grandfather, Attar Singh, was the founder of the Majithia clan. His son, Suran Singh, was a general in Ranjit Singh's army and fought in the Second Anglo-Sikh War against the British in 1847. A decade later, he was to fight alongside the British in the Mutiny of 1857, and was awarded vast tracts of land in the district of Gorakhpur, in the United Provinces. Umrao Singh, Amrita's father, was a truly remarkable man. A scholar of Sanskrit and Persian and a philosopher, he also dabbled in astronomy and carpentry. Many have credited him with being India's first modern photographer. Future generations have seen digitally reworked versions of his work through the archives of Amrita's nephew, the artist Vivan Sundaram, but a fuller understanding of his work is yet to happen. Amrita's mother, Marie Antoinette, was of Jewish and Italian descent and belonged to a well-to-do family in Hungary. Her father was a high-ranking government official. Marie Antoinette was extremely fond of music and played the piano very well, and it is said that it was during a piano recital that Umrao Singh instantly fell in love with Marie Antoinette and married her in Lahore in 1912. In the same year, the Sher-Gils set sail for Budapest, where Amrita was born; the very next year, in 1914, her sister Indira was born. Until 1921, the Sher-Gils were compelled to stay in Hungary due to the First World War. Umrao Singh, who by that point had stopped receiving regular 'aid' from India, was forced to move out to Marie Antoinette's family house in Dunaharaszti, on the outskirts of Budapest. It was there, living in those picturesque surroundings in a carefree world, that Amrita spent her childhood and first began to paint and draw with watercolours and crayons. Her cousin, Victor Egan, whom she later married, lived with her in the family home. He remembers the entire house as perpetually littered with Amrita's drawings. He noticed that she showed obvious signs of wanting to become an artist from a very early age.

In 1921, the Sher-Gils set sail for India, spending two weeks in Paris en route, where Amrita saw some of the world's greatest works of art for the first time, including the Mona Lisa. Her initiation had begun. Once in India, Umrao Singh acquired a house in Summer Hill, Simla, where Amrita began her early education. Although she flirted mildly with the piano, her deep and abiding passion was for painting. Recognizing this, Umrao Singh organized her first painting lessons at the hands of one Major Whitmarsh at first, and later by a Captain Petman, both of whom were her art teachers through the years 1924–27. Amrita's creativity and style began to flourish. Her talent and skill were noticed by her maternal uncle, Ervin Baktay, who happened to be visiting the family. He convinced them that Amrita had the potential to become a fine artist of great repute if she continued to receive regular professional training in art. He also taught her how to draw from live models, a practice Amrita continued throughout her life.

The young prodigy was admitted into the Ecole Nationale des Beaux-Arts in 1930, and began to paint with oils. She was drawn to the works of the impressionists, to Vincent

Van Gogh, Cezanne, Modigliani, and especially to Gauguin and his work on Tahitian women. Amrita made several portraits during this period, many of which are in collections in India, primarily at the National Gallery of Modern Art (NGMA) in New Delhi. Most of the research on Sher-Gil and her work during this period is restricted to the paintings that are housed in India, such as 'Man with Apples' (1932), 'Self Portrait' (1934), and the more well-received 'Young Girls' (1932), which won Sher-Gil a gold medal at school the very next year. The early works of Sher-Gil during this phase deserve far more attention than they have received so far. These works which were outside India seem also to have been outside of our comprehension and therefore analysis. Works such as 'Gypsy Girl from Zebegeny' (1932), which Sher-Gil painted while on vacation in Hungary, is a remarkably accomplished work for a young painter. Others, such as the tender portrait of her cousin whom she was clearly in love with at the time, 'Portrait of Victor Egan', also from 1932, deserve deliberate mention. Amrita's early self-portraits during that phase have never been reproduced or written about. It was during her years in Paris that Amrita Sher-Gil began to delve into her inner self, trying to explore her personal landscape and sexuality. Her bohemian life and free spirit allowed her, in Keats's words, '. . . to live a life of sensation'.

But all this did not meet with the approval of her father. Even though Sher-Gil was in love with her cousin, she had a series of affairs with men and perhaps a few relationships with women, became pregnant, underwent two abortions, and even contracted venereal disease from an Indian aristocrat. Through all this, her beloved, long-suffering Victor knew what was going on in her life.

By 1935, having mastered one style, she was yearning to

move beyond that, to push her own limitations. Amrita's 'romantic art' was hardly avant garde, and must have seemed a bit out of date in the Paris of the 1930s, which was entrenched in art deco, cubism and Bauhaus. Amrita realized that she would not be able to contribute much to the Modern art scene in Europe. Her strength lay elsewhere. She began to compare her India connection and relationship with that of Gauguin, who had painted women in Tahiti and Martinique. She made up her mind to reach out and discover her Indian side. She was also aware that there was no dominant figure in Indian art at the time, and that she could find an important place for herself 'back home'. Several years later she said rather vainly, 'Europe belongs to Picasso, Matisse and many others, India belongs only to me.'

It is noteworthy that Sher-Gil was confident of herself and her work only in a relatively unchallenged context. We know that she read Dostoevsky, Thomas Mann, D.H. Lawrence, James Joyce and Hungarian writers like Ady and Sazbo, and was not alien to radical thinking, but unfortunately, our comprehension of her taste and admiration in art stops at Impressionism. She never entered the realm of the avant garde of her time despite being as bohemian as one could get. In the latter half of 1934, at the age of twenty-one, Amrita returned to India. She sent ten paintings for the annual exhibition of the Simla Fine Arts Society, one of the most prestigious art exhibitions in the country at the time. Five were chosen and exhibited. Her works from this period began to absorb more from India. She wanted to interpret the lives of Indians, particularly poor Indians, whom she described as 'strangely beautiful in their ugliness'. Her technique and style stood apart—it was her very own, and had her unique stamp. Amrita's pictures were very well received during this exhibition, and one of them was awarded a gold medal. However, she caused a stir when she returned her award because she believed it had not been given to the right painting, the one that was acclaimed by critics in Paris. During this period she painted 'Mother India', 'The Beggars' and 'Hill Women', to name just a few. It was also during this year that she had an affair with Malcolm Muggeridge, the assistant editor of the Calcutta *Statesman*, the leading English language daily newspaper of the time. Amrita's first exhibition in Bombay was held the very next year at the Moorish Hall of the Taj Mahal Hotel. She was en route to South India with the great Bengal school painter, Barada Ukil, the brother of Sarada Ukil. This was probably the first time that her work was seen by all the influential people who were at the helm of the art scene in India, or connected with it in some way. Her work was lauded, and she got positive reviews in the press. One art critic who immediately responded to her work and later became a friend was Karl Khandalavala of the *Sunday Standard*. It was also during this exhibition that people like Dr Homi Bhabha, the noted scientist, saw her work for the first time. He was completely taken in by it. Dr Bhabha was later responsible for building one of the most important collections of Progressive painters for the Tata Institute of Fundamental Research. Interestingly, a young painter of billboards and hoardings, M.F. Husain, also saw Sher-Gil's work for the first time during this show. Karl Khandalavala, who was a keen and prodigious collector of miniature paintings, introduced Amrita to their fine composition and richness in colour. With Karl, she visited the Prince of Wales museum in Mumbai and was able to appreciate the beauty of Kangra and Basholi miniatures, which influenced her greatly in the years to come. During this same trip she visited the Ajanta and Ellora caves. Their scale and quality changed much for her, and the stupendous beauty and genius of the painters and sculptors who created these masterpieces centuries ago without the tools of a modern age overwhelmed her. She returned to the caves over and over again. 'I have, for the first time since my return to India, learnt something from somebody else's work,' she said. Ajanta and Ellora gave Amrita the Indian soul, identity and connectivity she yearned for. On the same trip she visited Cochin, Madurai, Trivandrum and Cape Comorin. The dark-skinned villagers, draped in white against the rich, emerald-green backdrop of a tropical land, made a strong visual impact on her work that followed. Back in Simla she made what were perhaps her most important pictures, best known as the South Indian trilogy: 'The Brides Toilet', 'The Brahmacharis' and 'South Indian Villagers Going to Market'. Gauguin's Tahiti and Sher-Gil's India had finally met. In these paintings Amrita had achieved the simplification of form and bold stylization that were distinctly her own. These works were indeed seminal, and over the years have come to symbolize the transition Amrita Sher-Gil underwent as well as the new direction that Indian art took thereafter.

In June 1938, Amrita left for Hungary to marry Victor Egan. She seemed to have temporarily severed her links with the 'Indian scene'. The few paintings she crafted in Hungary during that year were inspired by Brueghel the Elder in works such as 'The Hungarian Market Scene'. Sher-Gil seemed to have forgotten the India she once longed for, but not too long afterwards, political instability and the apprehensions of an impending war forced Amrita and Victor to return to India in 1939. After a brief sojourn in Simla, they moved to the Majithia family estate in Saraya, near Gorakhpur in Uttar

Pradesh. Although Saraya gave Sher-Gil all the comforts that a wealthy feudal household could provide, it offered her no intellectual impetus. She would spend time with the women around her, gradually becoming more aware of their social and psychological problems. As a result of those transient relationships, several of the pictures she painted during that time are about women within the immediate environs of her then habitat. Works such as 'The Ancient Story Teller', 'The Bride' and 'Woman Resting on Charpoy' were made during this phase in her life. They are amongst her best works. Amrita was always her own person, a young woman excited by exploration of all manner and kind. Influenced by her environment, friends and family, whether negatively or positively, Amrita managed to lead a full and controversial life in her few years. Her love for Victor was subliminal, one that she never questioned. Other lovers may have entered the fray and left, but one person did not replace the other. Her experiences were in the realm of hedonism and all her different relationships had their special niche in the canvas of her life. Just before her marriage to Victor, she discovered she was pregnant with someone else's child. Her husband discovered her condition only after they were married. Confronting this reality must have upset him no end, but he buried his own sadness and arranged for her to have a safe abortion. To quote her biographer, Yashodhara Dalmia, 'Real intercourse for Amrita took place at the level of ideas, where she was intensely and authentically involved and her thoughts could truly be fertilized by those of another. In this realm she did not hesitate to release a truly generative process. On the terrain that really mattered for her, there were many fruitful copulations.'

In 1941, Amrita went to Lahore with Victor, where she was to hold an exhibition. She suddenly fell ill on the night of 5 December, and abruptly passed away. The story of her life has been told through the eyes and memories of family, lovers, friends, critics, admirers, and through her letters to those she loved. I sometimes wonder if our understanding of Amrita Sher-Gil would be vastly different if we didn't have access to this written material. Would we be able to decode much of what she felt, thought and painted had it not been for her beautiful letters? What is more interesting is how over the years, circumstances have played a vital role in creating the Sher-Gil cult. In a museum starved nation, the fact that most of Sher-Gil's work is practically on permanent display at the NGMA has enabled generations of art lovers to fully absorb her genius in changing social contexts. To what extent does Sher-Gil's beauty and sexuality play a role in how we perceive her art? Or is it the art world's fascination with her untimely death that has put her on an international pedestal with legends like Van Gogh, Pollock and even Jean Michel Basquiat? There is no doubt that the fact that Sher-Gil shall remain perennially young and beautiful makes her an icon. Every time we think we know all there is to know about Amrita Sher-Gil, we are pleasantly surprised to discover yet another aspect of her life.

Vivan Sundaram has been involved with Sher-Gil's work for over thirty years as a curator, editor and archivist. From the large canvas titled 'The Sher-Gil Family' (1984) and the dramatic installation titled 'The Sher-Gil Archive in 1995', we recently saw 'Re-Take of Amrita' in 2001, an exquisite series of digital photomontages of the Sher-Gil family. For a collector, the fact that Amrita made approximately 150 paintings, most of which are in the NGMA and the rest with her family, makes her work virtually impossible to acquire.

Only a handful of her paintings lie in private collections, making her works as rare as those of Vermeer. Is it for these reasons that Sher-Gil is as famous as she is? Or is she the most important painter in India in the twentieth century? Perhaps the latter.

Conquering the Scale

Bhawana Somaaya

To understand a phenomenon, one needs to also understand the extraordinary circumstances that lead to its occurrence. If Lata Mangeshkar is a legend today, it has a lot to do with the extraordinary challenges she had to face in her early life.

Her father, Dinanath, was born near the Mangeshi temple to a Brahmin family, the Hardikars, who were natives of Goa. To protect the sanctity of the temple and preserve their old rituals from the Portuguese, Dinanath's father, Ganesh Bhatt Hardikar, began regularly performing the ritual *abhishek* in the temple. Hardikar, a respected leader in his community, took it upon himself to inspire a disciplined devotion that would retain unity within the community in the face of a Portuguese invasion. As he had initiated the custom of performing abhishek, the Hardikar family gradually came to be identified as 'Abhisheki', or caretakers of the Lord.

When Dinanath was eight years old, he ran away from home to escape the atrocities meted out to him by his stepmother. In a village far away from home, removed from the domestic troubles that he had left behind, Dinanath felt at peace and was reluctant to reveal his identity. His father was a respected man and Dinanath feared that if discovered, he would be sent back home. Young as he was, Dinanath understood the baggage of the family name and without further thought changed his surname to Mangeshkar, inspired from the family deity, Mangeshi.

Dinanath knew he would have to fend for himself, and the young boy joined a drama company as a chorus singer. The group travelled long hours on foot from one village to another, but despite many hardships, Dinanath never returned home. One day, Ganesh Bhatt learnt from some travellers that his son had become a successful singer and had started an independent drama company called the Balwant Drama Company.

Dinanath's company became fairly well known. He held frequent musical plays in all the neighbouring villages. During one such show held in Khandesh, a small town on the Gujarat-Maharashtra border, an elderly relative of Dinanath's suggested a marriage proposal for the singer. Narmada, the second daughter of the zamindar of Thadner, was so ravishing that Dinanath was mesmerized and agreed instantly. Narmada was only nineteen at the time; Dinanath, twenty-two. However, within just a few years of their marriage, Narmada fell mysteriously ill and passed away. As per the customs of the time, Dinanath was remarried to Narmada's younger sister, Shudhimati. Shudhimati bore Dinanath's five children—four daughters: Lata, Meena, Asha, Usha, and a son, Hridayanath.

Lata Mangeshkar was their first-born, and she arrived in the early hours of 28 September 1929. The city was Indore and the mood joyous. The Balwant Drama Company was flourishing, and Dinanath attributed his prosperity to his little Lakshmi, who he fondly addressed as 'Hridaya' (Heartfelt). There is an interesting story about how Lata first displayed her flair for music as a young child. Shudhimati had placed the little girl on the mattress on which Dinanath was in *riyaaz*. She asked her husband to mind the baby while she completed the household chores. Dinanath, like all artistes, was engrossed in his sarangi, when he suddenly noticed that Lata was emitting sounds in rhythm with the raag he was playing. He was overwhelmed—this was indeed a miracle. He became so emotional that he dropped his sarangi and ran inside the house to call out to his wife. 'We have an artiste amidst us, an infant who reacts to sur and taal . . .'

After that, Dinanath made it a practice to let Lata linger around him whenever he sat for his riyaaz. Perhaps it was then that the seed of love for music was sown. Lata Mangeshkar has often said that she grew up with the sound of music around her. 'The sounds of raagas and shlokas always reverberated in our home. For as long as my sisters and I can remember, Baba was all the time singing . . .'

Her earliest memories, Lata says, are in a small town called Yalner in Khandesh. 'My maternal grandmother lived there and I often visited her with Mai, my mother. Aaji had a small temple outside her home where all of us assembled in the evenings after dinner. She possessed an ancient harmonium on which she sang bhajans and *lavanis* to entertain all of us. She was a great storyteller and had a unique style of combining her narratives with songs . . . In all these years, I've never, ever encountered anyone with similar charm or talent. Though engrossed in domesticity from dawn to dusk, she was all the time singing. Interestingly, she had different songs for different activities, so it was a different mood when she was grinding the grain . . . ploughing the field . . . milking the cow . . . or cooking *puran-polis* for us grandchildren. Music followed Aaji like it belonged to her, and Aaji belonged to nature. Under the sky, beside the stream, she was forever singing and it was a voice that was not even formally trained.'

Dinanath was careful to begin his daughter's formal training in music when she was just seven years old. Every day, he would wake up Lata and her younger sister Meena at dawn to teach them music. 'If you learn in the mornings you absorb quickly,' he would always say, and it is a practice he followed till the end. 'He was a ruthless teacher and there were times we were not allowed to get up for hours at a stretch. Not even if Mai called us for food,' reminisces Lata. 'On such occasions we felt very martyred.'

The only other occasions on which the children felt deprived were when they were forbidden from watching films. Dinanath was vehemently against cinema. His children could not understand his ire, because his drama company was an extension of the same medium. But there was no arguing with Baba. But sometimes, when Dinanath was away on his long tours, Lata and her siblings would sneak inside a nearby film theatre and watch films. K.L. Saigal was a family favourite. These snatched moments were precious to them, and the enchanted images they saw on screen lingered long after the film was over. To recreate the aura, the sisters would re-enact the entire film, complete with songs and dialogues. 'It's amazing how we could remember every scene and every dialogue; every verse of every song. We never let our father know of our betrayal. Young as we were, we understood his anxieties,' reminisces Lata.

Dinanath Mangeshkar feared that the lure of films would distract them from their music. He feared that the glamour of show business would pollute their aesthetics. He had greater aspirations for his children, bigger dreams of mastery and purity in their chosen art. He wanted them to conquer higher notes, for he believed that films bred stagnation. His ambitions were manifold, but destiny had other plans.

In the years to come, the Balwant Drama Company ran into severe financial problems. To make matters worse, his troupe split up and his partners went their separate ways. To tide over the crisis, Dinanath announced a 'natya sangeet' in Sholapur. It was to be Lata's debut recital. Dinanath's colleagues were against it, but he had faith that Lata could stand on her own.

The show was a sell-out. As the nine-year-old raised her voice to the classical *'Shura mee vandile . . .'* ('I bow to thee, O brave Lord') from the popular play *Manapman*, the auditorium resounded with the sound of applause. Dinanath sat calmly while his colleagues looked at Lata, wonderstruck. When her performance ended, the little girl snuggled beside her father and fell asleep on his lap while still on stage, exhausted from the long hours of waiting.

Dinanath referred to Lata as his 'eldest son'. He always said that when he was no more, his beloved Hridaya would look after his drama company and his family. He began guiding her early for this mission, and she would accompany him for various festival programmes. This was a special time for her. During the journey, Dinanath would recount stories and recite songs to her, taking care to explain every note and every raaga. He was keen that his daughters were educated well, and sent them to a Sanskrit school. 'If you learn Sanskrit you learn all languages automatically,' he said.

It was a proud moment for him when one day he heard his three daughters recite the Gayatri Mantra. 'Come quickly!' he called out to his wife, 'These girls are messengers of God. Not only are their pronunciations perfect, but they are singing in perfect sur.' So overjoyed was Dinanath by their display of talent that he momentarily forgot his personal sorrows.

His drama company was on the verge of closure, as without funds it was difficult to keep the artistes together. His failure in business had affected his health and in frustration, Dinanath had resorted to drinking. It was something he was deeply ashamed of. When he was sober he would promise never to touch alcohol again, but he inevitably did, and the more he drank, the more arrogant he became.

In a few years, the family was forced to shift to Satara due to their financial condition. On the fateful night before Dinanath passed away, he called his daughters by his side. They were unsure of what to expect. In his feeble state, Dinanath asked them to sing for him. He could barely speak, but he handed his tanpura to Lata. 'I'm leaving you my notebooks of bandish,' he told her. 'Always keep these with you, and if you don't make the same mistakes I did, you will become a bigger artiste than I was.'

Lata was only thirteen at the time, and suddenly found herself responsible for her mother and four younger siblings. Gone were the days when she could roll rubber tyres down the streets or playfully steal guavas from the neighbour's orchard. 'So many times we were pulled up by Baba and got beaten up by Mai for the mischief. Mai would be so angry while hitting us that she often broke her glass bangles, but she would still not stop. After Baba passed away, we seldom troubled Mai and we seldom had fun.' Lata began working within a month of her father's demise. She nursed dreams of becoming a playback singer, but at thirteen her voice was not mature enough to be used for leading ladies. Much against her wishes, she had to settle for acting assignments in Navyug Films.

On the advice of a family friend, Lata agreed to act in a Marathi film co-produced by Master Vinayak. It was called *Pahili Manglagauri*. During the making of this film, Master

Vinayak fell out with his partners and launched his own independent company in Kolhapur. He wanted Lata to join him, but she could not as she was bound by contract. However, a year later, Lata joined Master Vinayak and did her first Hindi film, *Badi Maa*, starring Noorjahan. It was the opportunity of a lifetime. Lata admired Noorjahan, and one day in-between shots, she sang a few lines to Noorjahan from her film *Wapas*. Noorjahan was impressed. 'If you do your riyaaz seriously, you will become a great singer one day.'

As long as Dinanath was alive, Lata had received regular lessons in music from him. With her new routine it was becoming difficult to accommodate riyaaz into her frenzied schedule, but her commitment to her art was unwavering. No matter how late Lata returned from her shootings, she would reserve six hours every morning for riyaaz. She could not sing at home because it was a tiny room crammed with family and relatives, but there was a Shiva temple in the neighbourhood, similar to the one in her grandmother's village, and this is where Lata sought refuge. 'I would wake up at dawn and sing in the temple till sunrise . . . Then I'd go for a small stroll and return home rejuvenated to fight one more day,' says the songstress.

In those days, artistes were restricted to working with just one banner. Lata worked for a salary of sixty rupees a month for Navyug Films, but because Master Vinayak knew the Mangeshkar family he made a concession for Lata, allowing her to work for outside banners as well. The additional money was a great help, but the extra hours took a toll on the fragile girl. She hated putting on make-up, learning dialogues and facing the camera. 'It was all so artificial. Besides, that's not what I wanted to do.'

The day Lata was offered her first assignment as a playback

singer, she quit acting. 'It's not as if pursuing a singing career
was any less strenuous, but because it was something I wanted
to do, I was willing to face all the challenges.'

Her first playback assignment in Hindi came in 1947—
'*Aa lagu kar jori re*' by the music director Datta Davjekar in
Aap Ki Seva Mein. She was eighteen and raring to go. 'I was
on the threshold of a career and desperately seeking a guru.'
Deep down, there was a nagging fear that the guru would
overpower her previous learning from her father, but Ustaad
Amaan Ali Khan proved a magnanimous teacher. He
understood her anxieties and did not try and dislodge her
precious memories. He sensed she was undernourished, and
made it a point to carry fresh fruits and nuts for his student
whenever they met up for lessons. 'Also pakoras,' adds Lata
cheerfully. 'Guruji said chillies and fried stuff cleared the
throat. And it's true, because Baba never restrained his diet.'

Lata was slowly getting more and more singing
assignments, but their financial problems remained.
Unforeseen calamities struck the family from time to time,
and Master Vinayak's untimely demise was one of them. As
a family friend, Lata had trusted her mentor to preserve her
savings. Now with him gone, the family had fallen into bad
times again. 'The only thing that kept me going during that
low phase was my music. No matter how weighed down I
felt, when I sat down to do my riyaaz, I forgot the world.'
Every morning Lata boarded a train from Grant Road, where
they lived, to travel to Malad where Bombay Talkies was
situated. Singers had to rehearse a song for several days before
the recording. Also, there were two separate recordings—one
for the film, and the second for the HMV disc—but no extra
payments were made for these. In those days singers were not
mentioned in the credits, film titles or on record covers. The

first to protest and break this rule was Lata Mangeshkar, in Raj Kapoor's *Barsaat*, made in 1949.

How Lata Mangeshkar bagged the R.K. film is a story in itself. One day, a handsome boy arrived at Lata Mangeshkar's home with a message from Raj Kapoor. He wanted to meet her at his office the very next day. Lata assumed that the young man was Kapoor's assistant. The next day, when Lata landed up at the R.K. Films's office, she was shocked to find herself being introduced to the same young man who had visited her home—he was Raj Kapoor's new music director, Jaikishen.

That's where she met the rest of the R.K. regulars, like the music director Shankar and lyricists Shailendra and Hasrat Jaipuri. Gradually, the six of them became an inseparable gang that the rest of the film tribe admired and envied. They were constantly in each others' company, and enjoyed working together. During the music sittings and recordings, they had a lot of fun, and also lots of disagreements. 'We had a rule amongst us. Irrespective of who fought with whom, after every fight we made up with bhelpuri and ice cream at Chowpatty!' said Lata. The grapevine was full of their bittersweet anecdotes.

Starting with *Barsaat*, the Lata-Shankar-Jaikishen combination lasted all through the 1950s. But then during the making of *Sangam* in the early 1960s, Lata is believed to have had a disagreement with Raj Kapoor over the frivolous lyrics of the song '*Mein kya karoon Ram mujhe buddha mil gaya . . .*' After recording innumerable soulful numbers for films like *Shree 420* and *Awara*, she felt that Raj Kapoor had compromised on quality. Kapoor, however, disagreed. He felt the banter was necessary for the character, and this caused the first crack in their friendship. It was also around this time that Lata had a misunderstanding with Shankar, and they too fell out; then sometime in 1966, Shankar and Jaikishen stopped working together. However, Lata continued to sing for Jaikishen till he passed away in 1971.

More than a decade passed by. One day, Shankar dropped by unannounced at Lata's home. Lata was surprised, but didn't reveal it. He seemed troubled by his wife's illness. They talked of old times and old friends, but stayed clear of the topic of their old disagreement. After a few hours Shankar said, 'We will meet again, work together soon.' 'We will,' promised Lata. They came together again after a gap of twelve years in 1975, with *Sanyasi*. Several subsequent films followed—*Duniyadari, Garam Khoon* and *Papi Pet Ka Sawaal Hai*—but none left a mark.

Sixteen years after Jaikishen's demise, Shankar passed away in 1987. 'The loss was irreparable even though we had drifted away. How does one absolve memories of time spent together?' said Lata in an interview on radio.

The composers Laxmikant-Pyarelal were responsible for resolving Lata's split with Raj Kapoor during the filming of *Bobby* in late 1972. Laxmikant-Pyarelal were adamant that only Lata would sing their renditions. Deep down, both Lata and Raj Kapoor wanted to work together, but were too proud to make the initial overture. Laxmikant and Pyarelal sensed the situation and played the catalyst. When they began recording, it was obvious that both Lata and Raj Kapoor had missed the association. They were coming together after twelve years, and their reunion was a milestone moment for Hindi films. After *Bobby,* Lata continued to sing for all of Raj Kapoor's films, and even those made under the R.K. banner after his demise, including *Henna* directed by his son Randhir Kapoor and *Prem Granth* by Rajeev Kapoor.

Some years ago, when Lata released a double album called

Shraddhanjali, paying tribute to her deceased co-artistes and music directors, she said it was the music director Anil Biswas who had taught her the technique of inhaling and exhaling during singing. 'He taught me the art of fade-in and fade-out while holding a particular sur.' In her early days she was consumed by technique, but it was the maestro Ghulam Haider who made her appreciate the importance of feelings in words.

There is an oft-repeated story about how Dilip Kumar, who was introduced to her on a Mumbai local train, was initially dismissive of Lata because he was not convinced that a Maharashtrian could sing Urdu ghazals. Affronted by his remark, Lata swore to prove him wrong and hired a maulvi to work on her diction. After the immortal '*Aayega aane wala . . .*' from *Mahal*, Dilip Kumar accepted his mistake and remained her staunch admirer forever. On her part, Lata Mangeshkar has often said that no actor has rendered a classical song as effectively as Dilip Kumar in '*Madhuban mein radhika naache re . . .*' in the film *Kohinoor*.

It is said that the music director Naushad would make Lata rehearse every line in every song ten times before letting her near a microphone. '*Tod diya dil mera . . .*' in *Andaz* was okayed after twenty-eight takes. On the other hand, C. Ramchandra, most of whose chartbusters were made with Lata, 'usually okayed a song in the first take'. Different composers followed different methods but Lata blended with all; she had a personal equation with each of them. When S.D. Burman was satisfied with her rendition, he always made it a point to offer her a paan. Madan Mohan (whom she called 'Bhaiya') would merely play the harmonium, asking her to pick up whatever she liked.

She also had a knack for assessing talent. So whether it

was Kalyanji-Anandji in the late 1950s, Rahul Dev Burman and Laxmikant-Pyarelal in the 1960s, or Rajesh Roshan and Bappi Lahiri in the 1970s, they were composers who hit the headlines. Among the later composers, Lata has recorded for Raamlaxman, Anu Malik, Shiv-Hari, Anand-Milind, Nadeem-Shravan, Dilip Sen-Sameer Sen, Jatin-Lalit, Mahesh-Kishore, Shyam-Surender, Uttam Singh-Jagdish Khanna, Amar-Utpal, Jugal Kishore-Tilak Raj, A.R. Rahman, Aadesh Shrivastava, Vishal Bhardwaj, Nusrat Fateh Ali Khan, Adnan Sami and Rahul Sharma.

Lata Mangeshkar is the only singer privileged enough to have worked with virtually all the legendary singers and musical greats this country has produced, be it Mukesh, Mohammed Rafi, Kishore Kumar, Manna Dey, Talat Mehmood, Hemant Kumar or Mahendra Kapoor. In the next generation she has a full score with singers like Nitin Mukesh, Amit Kumar, Manhar, Bhupendra, Suresh Wadkar, Hariharan, Shailendra Singh, Anup Jalota, Talat Aziz, Anwar, Shabbir Kumar, Mohammed Aziz, Vinod Rathod, Roopkumar Rathod, Kumar Sanu, Jolly Mukherjee, Udit Narayan, Abhijeet, Sonu Nigam, Jagjit Singh, Yesudas and S.P. Balasubramaniam. She has also recorded over seventy-five songs with her sister, Asha Bhosle, and sung live with her other sisters Usha and Meena Mangeshkar, Suman Kalyanpur and Hemlata. In the following years she sang with Kavita Krishnamurthi, Ila Arun and Sulakshana Pandit.

Her biggest and best numbers, of course, were with Mohammed Rafi. Together, they were simply magical. Music directors were used to them outdoing each other at recordings, but it was always for the improvement of the song. Both were extremely focused, but sometimes the complexity of their relationship extended professional boundaries. In the later years, Rafi and Lata had a serious misunderstanding on a copyright issue and stopped singing together for three years, which was a major loss to film producers and more so to millions of their fans.

Despite new singers on the block and new and constantly evolving trends, she is the undisputed queen, the one consistent voice who has worked with seven generations of artistes, whose songs have been lip-synched by heroines from Nargis in the 1940s to Kareena Kapoor in the new millennium. She has cut albums of every genre in multiple languages, held live shows in scores of countries, has a perfume named after her, is the brand ambassador for a brand of diamonds, sponsors a hospital, and has an award instituted in her honour. She has been a Member of Parliament and has been awarded the country's highest civilian award, the Bharat Ratna. There is no dream she hasn't fulfilled, but no matter how high she flies, she remembers her father's words. 'If you are convinced that what you do is right, then you must . . . If you remain devoted to music, worship it without arrogance, it will absorb all your sorrows.'

If only Dinanath Mangeshkar were alive to see his daughter's glory.

Archiving the Nation

Sabeena Gadihoke

As a camerawoman starting out in the late eighties in relative isolation, I would often wonder about the absence of others in the profession until I saw a television news story about an older woman who had been a photojournalist when India became independent. As with many dream projects I had been associated with, my relationship with this extraordinary woman was to develop only when the time was right. It was 1998 when two projects—a film and a study on women photographers—coincided.

Homai Vyarawalla will be ninety-three in December 2006. She lives alone in Baroda. The city is not of her choice, but it is where she has lived for the past twenty-three years, far away from the vibrant life she enjoyed in Delhi for over three decades. The story of Homai's life starts almost a century ago, in 1913, when she was born to Dossabhai Hathiram, an actor in a travelling Urdu-Parsi theatre company and his second wife, Soonamai. Parsi theatre was very popular in those days, and it is even said to have laid the foundations for the Bombay film industry. Homai's father had acted in a few films, and while theatre held great fascination for his young daughter, it was not possible for girls from 'good families' to become actresses. Growing up in Bombay after the premature death of Dossabhai, Homai placed various options for a career before her orthodox mother. She wanted to be a doctor, and at one point even a Girl Guide, but fate determined that she would soon meet her future husband, Maneckshaw Vyarawalla, a self-taught photographer. Watching Maneckshaw experiment with his Rolleiflex camera, Homai picked up photography and was soon sending her images to magazines like the *Illustrated Weekly of India* and the *Bombay Chronicle*, but these were published under her husband's name.

Photography couldn't have stayed just a hobby, as Homai needed to earn a livelihood. Her middle class family had always faced financial hardship. They lived in Parsi mohallas quite removed from the affluent lives of others in their cosmopolitan community, which had marked its presence in Bombay through a long history of trade and entrepreneurship. From a fairly early age, Homai learnt to pay for her own education. She was always grateful to her mother for allowing her to do so, as Parsi women of her class faced several restrictions even if they were sent to school. Seeing her walk around with a camera—'Women in those days were not even supposed to carry a handbag'—people either made fun of her or ignored her. It was a mistake to underestimate her, as a government newsreel cameraman soon discovered. On assignment to cover the activities of the fire service for the *Illustrated Weekly of India* during the Second World War, Homai's stills of an explosion were published a week before his movie footage of the same event. 'She has killed my images!' he is said to have thundered, but it was too late.

Life was all set to continue in this vein, shooting festivals, cottage industries and utility services during the war, had it not been for the fact that Maneckshaw, whom she had married in 1941, unexpectedly got a job with the Far Eastern Bureau

(FEB), the publicity wing of the British Information Services in Delhi. Homai's career was to take a different turn when she too joined the FEB with Maneckshaw in 1942. This was an exciting time for a newly emerging group of news photographers in the capital. The events leading to Independence were unravelling in quick succession and Homai, as Maneckshaw's assistant, just happened to be in the right place each time. The lead-up to Partition, the first Independence Day speech at the Red Fort, cabinets being sworn in, visits of almost every important international dignitary to India, society weddings and receptions, dance performances, fancy dress parties at diplomatic missions— Homai covered them all. Her images of social functions were published in the *Onlooker* and *Current*. Social mobility was made possible by being featured on the pages of these magazines. She remembers how 'M.S. Oberoi once called up the editor of *Onlooker* enquiring, "Has she got something against me?" as his picture hadn't figured in the magazine!'

Homai's images of this time are a treasure trove of history, archiving a nation in transition. Her photographs might not have seemed significant to her then, but in retrospect some of them were to foretell key events that would challenge the new nation state, like the stunning images of a young Dalai Lama entering India for the first time in 1956, dressed in a brocade robe. She later photographed him flanked by Pandit Nehru and the Chinese premier Chou En-lai. These photographs, when viewed in retrospect, were portents of the simmering tension between India and China leading up to the war in 1962.

While her photography may have covered just three decades of independence, Homai's life spanned a much larger sweep of Indian history that marked the last days of the British

Raj, the excitement and euphoria of Independence, and disillusionment with its undelivered promises from the late 1960s onwards. She opted out of the profession at a time when the security surrounding Indira Gandhi was just beginning to make its presence felt. 'Distances between politicians and photographers became larger,' said Homai. The infamous 'licence raj' made it difficult for photographers to get their supplies of photographic material. Most of all, it was the beginning of the end of a certain cosmopolitanism and dignity that she associated Delhi with. It was just as well that Homai left her beloved Delhi for Pilani in 1970: she was spared the experience of seeing the city littered with posters during the Emergency, an event which was the culmination of her disillusionment with the promises of its rulers.

Homai's images of Dr Radhakrishnan, Lal Bahadur Shastri, Mahatma Gandhi, Abdul Kalam Azad, Dr Ambedkar and her favourite subject, Jawaharlal Nehru, are a testimony to the ease they felt with her. Citing the example of the photograph of Nehru wearing a cat's mask at a children's birthday party, the photographer Dayanita Singh observes that Homai's presence was not threatening to her subjects, and that they could relax in front of her. Being the only woman shooting at that time, she probably elicited unique responses from her subjects, who sometimes looked directly at her. Her ability to merge into the background also helped. 'You know I had developed lots of patience. Other photographers would always be in a hurry to finish off the photograph and get out . . . I would just go on watching and waiting. Waiting for the right moment, when they would not be conscious of the camera and be completely natural. Then I would just step forward, click and get out.' In her handling of all these pictures there was a strong sense of commitment to the subject, a belief in the essential dignity of those she photographed. This is documented in her reluctance to publish many of her photographs that portrayed her subjects in an undignified way. She asserts, 'They were comfortable with me because my pictures never offended anybody.' It is probably these attributes that marked Homai's work as different from that of her contemporaries.

There were no other professional women photojournalists in India in the 1930s, perhaps with the exception of the American Margaret Bourke-White, along with whom Homai recalls shooting Gandhiji's funeral at Birla House. Politics, like her chosen field of photography, was also almost completely male-dominated. Homai's colleagues at work were men, and she often had to travel unescorted on assignments all over the country. Surprisingly, she shared a comfortable relationship with most of her contemporaries and was a prominent (and the only woman) member of the News Cameramen's Association that they all started together. An extremely attractive woman, Homai cultivated a friendly but what she describes as 'no-nonsense' demeanour: 'There was no "hanky-panky" with me. If something went wrong, I would shout at the person and give him a good bang as well!' Interestingly, she was popularly known as 'mummy', a nickname that had been given to her by a colleague. She shrewdly notes that this 'kept her on a pedestal' and was perhaps a nickname that aided her. There are possibly other factors that helped too—her Parsi background, for instance, that marked her as different from other women journalists in the profession.

Despite her level of comfort with her colleagues, Homai Vyarawalla did not become one of the men. She was proud of the fact that she was the only woman photographer around and wanted this identity to be underlined. 'My idea is to keep one's identity as a woman because all along, for centuries, we have been taken for granted and people think we are incapable of doing anything. When we do a man's job, we must show them that it is a woman doing it and not men. I, being the only woman, wanted to keep my identity as a woman.' Despite suggestions that she should wear western attire, Homai cycled to work in a starched khadi sari with her cameras and paraphernalia slung across her slight frame. She also ran a home very efficiently and brought up her son to cook and to stitch his own clothes. Life in his growing-up years was a constant rush between the kitchen and the darkroom, which was in her pantry. She measured chemicals in much the same way as she measured spices in her kitchen, and seemed to enjoy domesticity as much as she enjoyed her profession. When she gave it all up in 1970, Homai turned into a homemaker for her son in Pilani. Cooking, gardening and an active member of the local women's club, Homai lived in Pilani for twelve years till she moved once again with her son to Baroda in 1982.

In an already invisible history of photojournalism in India, Homai's was a name that faded away; a self-imposed retirement far away from the limelight in Delhi, while her valuable images remained packed in trunks and boxes. She remained unaware of the significance of her own pictures till a Delhi-based photographer discovered her name among a list of men in the Press Information Bureau records. A spate of exhibitions and retrospectives, films and news stories followed, but Homai Vyarawalla remained completely untouched by the publicity. 'Mine has not been an extraordinary sort of life. It's just a normal kind of life that someone would want to live, but I had to work very hard.

Not that I resented it. On the contrary, I enjoyed that, because it gave me confidence to the extent that I could stand up to anything, any kind of work. Sometimes I would stay up for twenty-four hours, working without getting tired. Fortunately, providence gave me good health because of my simple life. There was nothing extravagant in anything I did. I like "simple, small and sober", and that has been the principle of my life all the time, and I think that kept me very much contented with myself.'

Celebrating Excellence

Leela Samson

Small beginnings, made in India's rural heartland, produced her most illustrious men and women. Rukmini Devi Arundale was born on 29 February 1904 in Madurai, Tamil Nadu to Neelakantha Iyer and Seshammal. Her father was an engineer with the public works department, and his work ensured that his family travelled extensively around the country with him. Of their eight children, Rukmini was the sixth-born.

As a child she was shy and introverted, but neither attitudes would be associated with her in later life. Her sister Visalakshi remembers her as a placid child, a clever mimic, an imaginative storyteller, and someone who loved to laugh. She was compassionate from an early age on, particularly towards animals and the meek or socially ostracized. During the family's travels through the Indian hinterland, as they halted at tiny villages to break journey in the evenings, Rukmini's father would read to her from the *Ramayana*. She would listen carefully, absorbing every detail, and began to take great pleasure in listening to the intonations of Sanskrit verse. Her mother's gentle voice in the kitchen influenced her love for the classical strains of the music of the Karnataka region. Her mother's knowledge of music was not shallow, and she sang raagas with a faith that had resonances in traditions beyond the audible.

When Rukmini was sixteen, her father moved to Adyar in Madras to spend his retirement years near the Theosophical Society. He was deeply influenced by the thinking of the leaders of the movement, and stirred by their spirit of nationalism, investigation and change. He was also interested in their reinterpretation of the Hindu scriptures. In the years to come, Neelakantha Iyer's family would give several generations of leaders to the Theosophical Society. His eldest son, Sri Ram, became the president of the Society, and to this day it is his granddaughter who heads it.

Among Sri Ram's many colleagues was the Englishman George Arundale. Brilliant, popular, jovial, and a theosophist like Sri Ram, he was one of Dr Annie Besant's most trusted lieutenants. Annie Besant, a heroine in the country of her birth, was a force to reckon with on the national scene in India's freedom movement as well. Before she left for India in 1893, there was no movement in the political and social life of England that she was not a part of, or in which she did not play a prominent role.

George Arundale's interest in Sri Ram's sister, Rukmini, created a scandal in the community. Nevertheless, he proposed and she accepted. When George and Rukmini decided to marry in 1920, he was forty-two and she was sixteen. An Englishman marrying the daughter of a vedanta scholar and high class Brahmin—as expected, it raked up a storm. The controversy stirred the passions of the conservative Brahmin community of which she was a part, and became a public issue. The couple's decision was difficult to support, both for Annie Besant as well as for Rukmini's recently widowed mother. Opposition to the marriage was vehement, and Sri Ram too found it difficult to back his sister, as he admired Annie Besant greatly.

While the support of her family was crucial to the young girl, the difficulties she faced brought out her determination. She had lived in the interiors of Tamil Nadu, only just lost her father, and recently moved to the city of Madras. Besides, she was only sixteen years old. Yet she had it in her to brave the storm of tremendous opposition to her intended marriage, especially from within her own family. The couple went to Mumbai, and on 27 April 1920, in a simple, quiet ceremony, Rukmini and George Arundale were married by the Registrar of Civil Marriages.

Like many a storm, this too subsided as quickly as it had begun. It seemed like destiny had brought them together. He was a devoted husband, a natural teacher, both caring and youthful in spirit. Her education in Western and Indian culture had just begun, and she was a quick learner. The couple were deeply committed to the Theosophical movement—he was interested in education and involved in the practical and administrative work of the society, while she was attracted to the philosophical dimension. Before she married George Arundale, Rukmini's knowledge of English had been minimal. Besides the language and etiquette of the new, upper class society they now lived amidst, there was much to learn in the intellectual sphere in which he worked.

The early opposition to her marriage seems to have been a sign of things to come. She would have to face many such hurdles in her life, and in facing each of these she was guided by a philosophy—an 'inner spirit' is how she described it. While talking about her marriage in 1936, sixteen years later, she said, 'No matter what our convictions are, we cannot judge people, cannot expect them to live by our understanding of life. The real spirit of marriage is an ideal. You must immerse yourself, your spirit in it, in order to know what it is. We must each live according to our own ideal, something apart from the law of the land, which makes marriage the result of one's inner life. We must live the life which is beyond the physical, which finds its true expression through the physical.'

After they were married, Rukmini and George lived in Indore, Madhya Pradesh, where Maharaja Holkar had asked George to take charge of education in the state. George had first come to India in 1903 at the request of Annie Besant. She needed a professor of history for the Central Hindu College, Benares, where he taught until 1912, after which he left for Adyar, the headquarters of the Theosophical Society. 'If education were for living and not merely for livelihood; if education were for joy and happiness and not merely for temporal success; if education were for self-expression and not so exclusively for imitation; if education were as much for eternity as it is for time; if education were as much for wisdom and truth as it is for so-called facts; if education were as much for the soul as it is supposed to be for the mind; then indeed would the younger generation be well-equipped for life.' It is with these words and this philosophy that George took up his task in Indore.

A few years later Annie Besant called them back to Adyar, where they worked relentlessly and vigorously for the reconstruction of the country. Annie Besant spoke out for independence from British rule, and worked hard to influence the British government to give it back to the people of India. Her voice was a force that Gandhiji understood well—he knew its influence upon England. She had trusted workers, both within the Theosophical movement as well as in the rest of the country. C. Jinarajadasa, Sri Ram, Telang, Trilokekar and several others, apart from numerous followers all over the world, were involved in the movement with her.

In 1923, George Arundale helped start the Young Theosophists Movement in India. Rukmini became the president of this society, and with this her work in the theosophical sphere began. There was much to be done in the areas of education, art, philosophy, politics, social work and animal welfare. Annie Besant believed that the Theosophical Society could do much to contribute towards these various facets of freedom at this crucial time in India's history. She also believed that the Society could influence the other nations of the world against the British domination of India.

In 1924, Annie Besant sailed for England with the Commonwealth of India Bill, the result of three years' laborious work by a number of Indian patriots who desired to have it placed before the British parliament. It was meant to be a Constitution for India, by the Indians. This coincided with a remarkable public meeting at the Queen's Hall, London, on 23 July of that year to celebrate fifty years of Mrs Besant's contribution to public life. Rukmini was only twenty. It was her first journey across the oceans, and must surely have been a memorable one, travelling as she was in such illustrious company.

The Theosophical Society was itself in the throes of huge change that year. Jiddu Krishnamurti, his deep love for Mrs Besant notwithstanding, had denounced his belief in religion and the spiritual masters, and had described all rituals as 'crutches'. A split was imminent among the followers of the movement. Power equations were changing, and despite the fact that the members were followers of both Krishnamurti and Mrs Besant, it was inevitable that they would take sides. Rukmini and George Arundale were no doubt caught up in this turmoil. In fact, George Arundale had tutored

Krishnamurti and his brother, Nityananda, while they were studying in Europe.

The effect of the split in the Theosophical movement as a result of Krishnamurti's departure and later the death of Annie Besant can never be fully assessed. Many feel it broke the back of the movement, and that it was never quite the same again. Nevertheless, within the broad parameters of the work of the Society, Rukmini's responsibilities had become more defined. She enthused members of the Society with her love for artistic expression and her youthful spirit. Several of them got together and formed a theatre group called 'The Adyar Players'. They wished to promote the artistic and creative life of the Society. Proceeds from their efforts went towards animal welfare work, which was dear to them all, and especially to Rukmini. As a member of independent India's Rajya Sabha, she helped formulate the Prevention of Cruelty to Animals Bill, the pioneering legal guideline that would serve to protect animals against their 'protector', man.

Annie Besant would enthusiastically participate in the artistic efforts of the Society, once even rendering a portion of Tennyson's epic poem *Idylls of the King*. For a while their dramatic rendering of Longfellow's *Hiawatha* and Sir Edwin Arnold's *The Light of Asia* became much anticipated features at the Society's annual conventions. These forays into the magic and intricacies of the stage were an important phase in Rukmini's learning curve, who was the soul of these presentations. She experimented with Egyptian, Hungarian and South American dances, using what talent was available among the members, often choosing the most unseemly members of the society to act in these performances! It must have been terribly amusing, for those chosen were selected more for their temperament and demeanour rather than any acting skill. They were Theosophists first, and what they sought to express on stage was an articulation of their ideals, not mere entertainment.

It was in 1929 that Rukmini, en route to Australia with her husband, found herself occupying the cabin opposite the legendary Russian dancer, Anna Pavlova. Her life was to change as a result of that meeting, and although Pavlova was elusive, her own curiosity about this graceful Indian woman led to a lasting friendship. An attractive Englishman with a beautiful, young Indian wife by his side—the couple were as much the cynosure of all eyes onboard the ship as Pavlova and her troupe of forty dancers were! Their admiration for each other grew. In Australia, Pavlova arranged for ballet lessons for Rukmini, who was fascinated by her performances. When she returned to India, she sought out dance recitals in Madras. She saw every good dancer of the time perform and in December 1932, she witnessed a Sadir performance by the renowned Pandanallur sisters, Rajeswari and Jeevaratnam. Bharatanatyam, the classical dance of Tamil Nadu, was then known as Sadir. She determinedly sought her way to their guru, the doyen of the Pandanallur style, an upright and elderly gentleman called Meenakshi Sundaram Pillai.

In September 1933, Annie Besant passed away. Nine months later, George Arundale was voted president of the Theosophical Society. He was fifty-five and his wife only twenty-nine. The Society was by now a forceful body of thinkers with a worldwide membership. Its publications were (and still are) among the best on philosophical thought. In 1934, George and Rukmini started a school based on Theosophical principles in Adyar, in memory of Annie Besant. With it began Rukmini's work in the field of education.

Attached to it was a cultural centre, which together with the school began imparting the kind of education that people now dream of for their children. It grew simply, with the highest ideals, bringing together the best of Indian thought and philosophy. It eschewed the worst traditions of British education like punishment and the well-known lack of attention to the great traditions of Indian learning. Fees were kept low. Vegetarianism was made compulsory. No punishment, in any form, was allowed to be perpetrated. 'Self government' was the principle adopted by one and all.

Meanwhile, Rukmini Devi had begun to excel in Sadir. On 30 December 1935, she invited doubters, sceptics and the interested alike for a performance of the dance. E. Krishna Iyer, a Brahmin gentleman who was responsible for the revival of the dance we now know as Bharatanatyam as well as for the rehabilitation of the traditional performers, devadasis, into respectability, found an ally in Rukmini Devi. He encouraged her to become one of the first women of their community to perform the dance, which had fallen into moral disrepute. What followed was a revolution. Even the ultra-conservative were converted, and those who had no idea of the dance's worth began to look at it as a truly beautiful art form; from a fresh perspective. The tide of prejudice which had existed against Sadir was to turn after her performance. The confidence and conviction with which she simply did what she saw as beautiful and pure, with absolute resolve and without a trace of apprehension about the potential stigma, was her lasting contribution to the culture of south India. If Bharatanatyam is accepted as one of the most important classical dance forms in India today, it is in no small way due to her contribution and participative support. Her performance was acclaimed to be outstanding in its aesthetic appeal, its altered presentation and choice of items. She was dedicated, and sought to express a 'spiritual' or 'inner' connection with her art, till then not attempted by her contemporaries.

On 6 January 1936 she started another cultural revolution. She put her mind to teaching children about the beauty of the arts and crafts of south India. Alongside the Besant Theosophical High School, she built a cottage to teach Sadir to anyone who would send their children to her to learn. At first the arts school was called the International Academy of the Arts, but very soon it was renamed Kalakshetra. She persuaded her own guru, Meenakshi Sundaram Pillai and other stalwarts of dance and music to come and teach in Kalakshetra. Many of them had been neglected by society, and happily accepted her invitation to do something they had never done before, that is, taught in a school. They were traditional gurus, legendary figures who almost no one in nationalist India knew or cared about. They became Kalakshetra's first teachers, and she their first pupil.

Her enthusiasm and vision were constantly expanding. Nothing seemed out of place in her world-view of 'connectedness' to the whole. When she saw the traditional craft of weaving in despair, she started a crafts centre for weavers so that they might revive the traditional Temple sari. In 1939 she and her husband invited Madame Maria Montessori to India, bringing the possibility and promise of alternative systems of education, something Indian nationalist leaders were not even thinking of at the time. Apart from her involvement in dance and the school, she was a vociferous advocate of vegetarianism, and would go to the surrounding villages with her small band of followers in bullock carts, singing bhajans against animal slaughter in temples.

Her mission was clear. But many others in the Theosophical Society were not sure whether these activities were truly 'theosophical' in nature. There was also speculation about whether they were not bringing one person too much attention. She was the president's wife, and perhaps she ought to pay more attention to the duties of that post, said some. A feeling that the president indulged her was not least among their grudges, and soon a policy of disassociation with Rukmini Devi and her activities began to manifest itself. She was, after all, operating these institutions on land owned by the Theosophical Society, and depended on the Society for the various facilities that were required to operate these schools. The sad demise of George Arundale on 12 August 1945 put a lid on the issue. In the following years, the different projects she was involved with came to be suspected as having an ulterior or selfish motive. By 1947 the boycott of her activities became a reality, however gentle its persuasion may have seemed on the surface. This was one of the great disappointments of her life.

However, she overcame these hurdles and soon took control of her schools and situated them on lands a few miles further down the coast from Adyar. Although she continued to remain an important member of the Society till she died, the hurt remained, and she was bewildered by the hostility of her co-members. She never quite understood why good work in education or art was considered 'non-theosophical'. In her lifetime it would become clear that it was not her work, but her, that they objected to.

Rukmini Devi never allowed herself to be derailed by the problems or obstacles that came her way, and continued with her work. People would come to her with scripts that she would choreograph into what she referred to as 'dance dramas'. She became intricately associated with the development of this genre. Using the great Western ballets as examples, she became a master at the art and craft of storytelling. Her narration was accomplished with great sensitivity to the Indian context. It is often called *purva janam vaasanai*, or the memories or scent of a past life. For my generation these dance dramas were a work of genius—no one had done anything quite like it before. For although dramatic dance-art like Koodiyattam, Kathakali, Bhagavatha Mela and Manipuri existed, choreographed versions did not exist at the time. She put her mind to bringing the solo art of Sadir on to the proscenium stage, but with a difference. She used a group of dancers to depict and connect abstract moments in the dance drama, taking the story forward on their strength and creating a new avatar of the art. The solo format was clearly another form. To this, too, she added vocabulary and made sweeping reforms in costume, presentation, musical accompaniment and text. The culmination of all these dramas, each different in character and scope, borrowing from different textual traditions and in at least five languages, was a six-part rendition of Valmiki's *Ramayana*. In these works she had the collaboration of several stalwart musicians of the time, such as Mysore Vasudevachariar, Tiger Varadacharya and his brother Krishnamacharya, Papanasam Sivan and a host of others. She was also assisted by a panel of scholars, each one an expert in a particular language or familiar with a particular text. Her students were by now well trained, and with her directorial touch they rose to deliver adept performances and sculpt characters that still live in the memory of a growing and devoted audience.

In 1952, the President of India nominated Rukmini Devi Arundale to the Rajya Sabha for her services to Indian culture.

It was an honour she gracefully accepted. Years later, she became the first woman to be offered the position of the President of India, which was an even greater honour. This, she politely refused. Her work in parliament proved to serve the causes of animal welfare and women, the Tibetan cause and her lifelong work in the field of education more than the arts, which is the field that people generally associate her name with. She was an early supporter of the Tibetan cause, the first to take Tibetan refugee children into her schools, where they stayed until they made their way in the world through high school, college or employment. To the new art bodies she would say, 'Why do you preserve art? Preserving is useful, but preserving the artists is more useful. Propagating art is vital. Help the artists and their art will be preserved naturally.' They did not like her very much and were grudging of her special place in the scheme of things. So vital was her message that ignoring her was not possible. However, preaching was not her style—she was a woman of action.

Vegetarianism and the cause of animal welfare took her worldwide, and she fought against the vivisection of monkeys for research, the game of bullfighting in Spain, advocated the betterment of the methods of slaughter in India, and spoke out against animal sacrifice in temples. She was instrumental in passing a bill in parliament that was crucial to our understanding of ahimsa. India was exporting animals for experimentation to laboratories abroad at a time when conditions for their travel were pathetic. Hundreds of monkeys died on these journeys. Indian slaughter houses were, according to her, 'living hells'. Cattle farms, medical research laboratories, vaccine institutions, veterinary colleges, livestock and research stations, circuses and zoos— she visited them all and spoke out for a policy that would protect the helpless animals which were being used in them. 'Does man believe foolishly that animals were created for him and his pleasure alone?' she asked. 'When I was nominated to parliament I thought I would be a voice for the animal kingdom. My greatest joy has been to bring their cry of hope to our leaders.'

To her many pupils in Madras she became a mother, a strict disciplinarian who demanded the highest effort and purity of form from them. She had influential friends, but it was the creative ones whom she brought to meet the students—clairvoyants, yogis, mendicants, scholars, philosophers, scientists, artists—non-conformists of every hue became regular visitors. They would talk about their worlds. Many of them had lived very unusual lives, and it was truly amazing to interact with them. These little diversions in the timetable of school life made her students understand who she really was.

Beauty at all levels, in all forms, was a passion. She deplored 'unmindful' acts of piety, yet made ritual elegant. She was loved by many, admired by even more. All the great leaders of her time were personal friends—Jawaharlal Nehru, in whose tenure she served in parliament; his daughter, Indira Gandhi, who was a personal friend; Dr Radhakrishnan; Sir C.P. Ramaswamy Iyer; Sri Sadasivan and M.S. Subbulakshmi; Kalki Krishnamurthi and numerous others. She was a good friend, outspoken and committed to a cause, yet pliable when it came to family and her institutes.

She abhorred the idea of asking for financial support, yet when it came from well-wishers she was grateful. Those who worked closely with her had no interest in money. They were Theosophists, and work was their life. Her own understanding of money was negligible; so too that of her constant and loyal companions, Sankara Menon, Dr Padmasini and

Kamala Trilokekar. She knew the value and necessity of money for the work she wanted to do, but had no idea how to handle it. She could prove to be naive, and would often allow the wrong people to guide her.

Kalakshetra's golden jubilee celebrations were celebrated with great joy in December 1985. Having lived a full life, Rukmini Devi Arundale passed away in February 1986. She was criticized for not leaving behind a successor, but Sankara Menon, her erudite and scholarly right-hand man, an aristocrat and a gentleman, took over the institute and ushered it into a new phase of stability. Aware that many unscrupulous people were eyeing the institute's land and sensing pressure from these sources to take over the academy, he handed it over to the Central government in 1993 just before his death. Today, Kalakshetra is an autonomous organization, run by an elected governing body that assists in advising and informing its work through the expertise of its members. It has been declared an 'institute of national importance' by an act of parliament, granting it autonomy to preserve and propagate the arts for future generations, just as its founder would have wished.

The Adivasi Mahasveta

Ganesh N. Devy

D o I know Mahasveta Devi ? Perhaps, I do; perhaps not. In the early 1980s I launched a journal of literary translations, and was keen to have a Mahasveta Devi story for it. I wrote to her, and she sent her own translations of 'Death of Jagmohan, the Elephant' and 'Seeds'. The manuscripts looked uninviting: close type in the smallest possible font size on sheets smudged with blue carbon. The stories were great, for their authentic realism and sharpness of political analysis. I knew that she had written about the kind of India that is mine.

After they were published, I sent her two money orders of Rs 50 each as an honorarium. She promptly returned the money, requesting that it be used as a 'donation for whatever work you are doing'. In the years that followed, I never met her at literary gatherings; not even in Kolkata, where she lived. Once I was in Kolkata on a literary call. When I asked friends about the whereabouts of 'Bortika', which I thought was the name of a locality, they were quick to point out that Mahasveta did not like academics. I was clueless as to how I could get to meet her.

In the mid 1990s I decided to give up academic life and enter the world of the adivasis. The organization founded by me together with some friends for this purpose was called

'Bhasha' to represent the 'voice of the adivasis'. Since the work was to be in remote adivasi villages, my colleagues felt that we should institute an annual lecture on adivasis in Baroda. We decided to name it after Verrier Elwin.

Every time we started shortlisting speakers for the Elwin lecture, Mahasveta Devi's name would come up first. But I had no idea how to get such a renowned person to Baroda, or even whether she would be interested in giving a lecture. The Jnanpith and Magsaysay awards, given to her in 1996–97, only made things more difficult for me. Nevertheless, I sent her a letter of invitation. She did not respond.

In January 1998, I was at the India International Centre (IIC) in Delhi to meet the noted playwright Chandrashekhar Kambar. I ran into Dinesh Mishra, the then director of the Jnanpith Foundation, who offered to introduce me to Mahasveta Devi. We went up to her room and as introduction, he said some kind words about me. She looked at me once, and said that she would accept the invitation to Baroda, but gave no date. She then looked up again. I knew that my time with her was up.

In February 1998, Professor Amiya Dev, the vice-chancellor of Vidyasagar University, invited me to Midnapore for a seminar. I travelled to Bengal, this time with a team of ten adivasi writers and storytellers. I was unaware till we reached the university that Mahasveta Devi was to speak at the seminar. It was the first time I heard her speak. I did not follow all of what she said, because she looked disturbed, speaking with pain and anger. We requested Professor Amiya Dev to arrange a meeting with her, but since she was to leave for Kolkata the same evening, we were given only fifteen minutes. I barely managed to introduce my colleagues, including Bhagwandas Patel, the great folklorist, and the celebrated Marathi writer, Laxman Gaikwad. She did, however, give a definite date for the Elwin lecture in Baroda.

The Elwin lecture was to be in March. Mahasveta Devi chose to speak on the 'Denotified Tribes of India' (DNTs). Our practice was to combine the Elwin lecture with a major seminar. That year, we had more than fifty adivasi delegates from all over India. I had arranged to take them to an island in the Narmada, some 90 km south of Baroda, on the same day that Mahasveta was to arrive. Since I could not receive her at Ahmedabad airport, 115 km north of Baroda, I requested my activist friend, Ajay Dandekar, and Tridip Suhrud, a friend and former student, to do so and bring her to Baroda.

I returned from the island quite late. They reached Baroda even later in the night. I had asked them to dine en route, before dropping her at the guest house where she was to stay. Throughout their journey from Ahmedabad to Baroda, I kept receiving calls from them, telling me that Mahasveta seemed upset; that she was refusing to eat. So I suggested they bring her home. My wife was not in Baroda. I had not eaten, nor did I know if there was food at home. When Ajay and Tridip arrived, they showed clear signs of some strain. I had no idea how to greet her, and so I asked, 'Do you have your own teeth?' I do not think anybody had ever asked her anything so rude. My intention was to figure out if she would be able to chew the few slices of hardened bread that I was planning to offer her with some pickles and onion.

On hearing my question she burst out laughing. She laughed so hard that my neighbours, waiting behind the windows to have a glimpse of the celebrity, came out in curiosity. We had an impromptu meeting across the fence, and she spoke to each one of them with great affection. They rushed into their kitchens, cooked, and brought dal and rice for her, which she happily ate. We talked, and I made endless cups of tea for her. She offered to stay in my simple house. When I apologized for its simplicity, she said, 'This is luxury for me. You should see my house in Kolkata.'

I asked her why she had decided to call it Bortika. She laughed again and said, 'You have no brains, it is not the name of my house, it is the journal that I bring out.' *Bortika* had been so named by her father, who had founded the journal. 'Bortika' or 'vartika' literally means 'narratives' or 'reports'.

I poured more tea for her. By now, our other colleagues whom I had packed off for the night in the two small rooms upstairs, joined us. She started telling us about herself, beginning with the famous 'non-vegetarian cow', about her father and mother, her childhood, the brief stay in Shantiniketan, her very special views on Rabindranath Tagore and Bengal, and how she started work as a roving journalist, bringing to light the conditions of bonded labour and adivasis.

She spoke at length about Palamu, about her adventures collecting material on Laxmibai of Jhansi, about how she lost the Jnanpith award cheque given to her by Nelson Mandela. We all knew that she had found in our gang of writer-activists a company close to her heart. She told me how, when I went to see her at the IIC, she had thought that I was a zamindar's son because I was wearing a clean shirt. By the time the clock struck four, our friendship was sealed. She was 73; I was 48; the youngest of my colleagues was barely 23. We knew we were all one.

Her Elwin lecture was deeply moving. She had no written script, and spoke of the civilizational graces of the adivasis, of how our society had mindlessly destroyed the culture of our great continent, and how these innocents had been brutalized. She described the context in which the infamous Criminal Tribes Act, 1871 had been introduced, the process of denotification in 1952, and the plight of the nomadic communities in India ever since. The denotified tribals are human beings too, she implored. She then narrated the gruesome episode of the custodial death of Budhan Sabar in Purulia in February 1998, a day before we first met her at the Vidyasagar University. At that time she looked shattered, deeply agonized, but I did not know the country of pain she was inhabiting on that day in Purulia.

The word 'spellbound' is inadequate to describe the effect she had on her audience. The utter simplicity of her bearing, the sincerity conveyed through her body language, and her direct style, defeating all grammar, had completely overwhelmed the audience. Here was a no-pretence, no-rhetoric, no-nonsense person, whose compassion and clarity were an invitation for action. Perhaps Mahatma Gandhi alone, among great Indians, spoke like her.

The next morning, several of my young students and colleagues came home to meet her and listen to her. Some of them brought food, which we all shared. In the afternoon I asked her if she was prepared for a trek out to Tejgadh, a good 90 km from Baroda. She was more than willing to undertake the journey. That afternoon I showed her the location of the Adivasi Academy I was struggling to create in Tejgadh, and the 12,000 year old rock paintings in the nearby Koraj hill.

We then trooped off to a stream which met the Orsang river and all of us, Mahasveta included, had a dip. She was only 73. She said, 'I have not been here before, but I have seen this rock-painting a long time back. I have seen the Pithora painted in my adivasi friend from Tejgadh, Nagin

Rathwa's house a long time back. Read my "Pterodactyl". I recognize this voice. It is beyond time.' She added, 'Do you know about the Saora paintings? They no longer have figures in the same form, but the adivasi memory never forgets.' I knew that, yet again, Mahasveta Devi had found in Tejgadh the timeless voice and the indestructible memory that made the adivasis what they are. This discovery was the beginning of a long journey for both of us. The next day, in Baroda, we formed the Denotified and Nomadic Tribes Rights Action Group, the DNT-RAG. The day she left Baroda, I fractured my foot.

Even before the plaster had been removed I was with Mahasveta Devi again, this time in Hyderabad, from where we travelled to Warangal. The Malayalam novelist, P. Sachidanandan, and the literary scholar, Jaidev, were also with us. Mahasveta Devi spoke of her activist life; I about her literary work. We returned to Hyderabad to hold a press conference and address a gathering of activists on the DNT question. We then went to Mumbai where, along with the writer Laxman Gaikwad, we met the deputy chief minister of Maharashtra. He was keen that Mahasveta Devi address the Marathi Literary Conference.

She spoke to him about human rights violations in Mumbai. I had by now observed that she spared no one, in particular snobs, ministers, insincere journalists and literary aspirants. During that meeting I was informed that my teacher, the Kannada fiction writer Shantinath Desai, had passed away the previous day. I wanted to be with his family. Mahasveta Devi declared that she would brave the 300 km overnight road journey with us to Kolhapur, where he lived.

We travelled; she remained absorbed watching the red sky, typical of the Western Ghats, through the long hours of sunset. She told Laxman and me about the time when she was very young, newly married and looking for material support for the family. A friend told her that exporting monkeys would be a lucrative business, and promised to help her. But when she learnt that this would be illegal, she lost her nerve and decided to release an army of young monkeys near Khandala. This was when she lived in Mumbai with her husband, who played a prominent role in the Indian People's Theatre Association (IPTA) movement, and had a brush with the world of Hindi cinema. She talked of the singer Hemanta Kumar Mukherjee with the same ease as she did about Ernest Hemingway and Arthur Miller, about Madhubala as of Sadat Hasan Manto; all her great favourites.

Mahasveta, more a woman of film songs than of raagas, of laughter than long-faced pontificating, is closer to that which reveals than that which decorates and conceals. And yet she is completely detached from everything. You cannot please her by praise or by providing her with creature comforts. She is almost not there when one thinks she is very much there.

Soon we found ourselves together in Delhi. This time the National Human Rights Commission had responded to our letter about the denotified tribes issue. The Commission appointed a committee to prepare a report. We visited Delhi on several occasions in order to complete the report. Every trip meant meeting more people, addressing press conferences, campaigning with greater energy. We met people at the Election Commission, the census authorities, the home minister, the welfare minister, former prime ministers, MPs, journalists, addressed gathering at press clubs, university hostels, colleges and institutions. In between these trips we were in Maharashtra, making long overnight journeys to places like Ahmednagar, Yavatmal, Latur, Sholapur, Dhulia,

Jalgaon and Baramati. At these places we met with the Pardhis, Wadars, Bhamtes, Bairagis and Kaikadis. We went to police stations to lodge complaints of rape, torture and humiliation, often against those whose job it was to protect people. We visited the sites of old and fresh atrocities.

Mahasveta brought to those poor and harassed people a boundless compassion, which they instantly understood, though they could neither speak her language, nor she theirs. She has a strange ability to communicate with the silenced, her best speech reserved for those to whom no one has spoken.

Between visits to Delhi and travels in Maharashtra, she made frequent trips to Gujarat. Baroda became her second home; Tejgadh her sacred grove for communion with the adivasis. 'In Tejgadh alone,' she said, 'my bones will find rest. Ganesh, you will understand, I am tired of it all, this praise, this deification. I hate it.' In Gujarat, she went everywhere, to the villages of Panchamahals with the poet Kanji Patel, to the mournful ex-settlement of the DNTs in Chharanagar, Ahmedabad, and Khedbrahma to meet the singers of the Garasia-Bhil *Mahabharata*.

When Budhan was killed in police custody in Purulia, Mahasveta Devi had filed a case in the Kolkata High Court. The judgement ordered compensation to Budhan's widow, Shyamali. By the time this judgement was delivered by Justice Ruma Paul, Mahasveta Devi and I had already started our work at Chharanagar. We established a library there, for which she donated the amount received by her as the first Yasmin award.

Chhara boys and girls, whose parents had been branded thieves by the rest of the world, found in her a great pillar of support and strength. They started calling her 'Amma', as thousands of adivasis in India had done. They composed a play on the life and death of Budhan and performed it before her during the first national convention of the denotified tribes held in Chharanagar on 31 August 1998. In the play, she was depicted as a character who pleads for the dignity and rights of the denotified tribes in the Kolkata High Court. She cried as she watched the agony of the branded through the play.

Mahasveta Devi discovered for herself three places of rest in Gujarat: Tejgadh, with its timeless memory and the mysterious voice of its adivasis; Chharanagar, with its intricate imagination of Indian criminality and spirituality; and the artist Bhupen Khakhar's house in Baroda with its 'forensic' approach to sentimentality. Bhupen had long been a friend, and I thought she would take to him gracefully as a friend's friend. Their first encounter was not pleasant. She scolded him for not engaging in direct social activism. Bhupen, with his typical humour said, 'Ganesh Devy is an activist. I paint.'

But soon they were friends, as profound a friendship as has ever been. I knew that both belonged to a different league, akin to Gandhi and Tagore. Every time they were together she would sing for him a Suraiya or Noorjahan number, but mostly *More baal-pan ke saathi* ('O, companion of my childhood'), and Bhupen would sing for her a few Gujarati bhajans. Both sang with a fullness of their selves. She never failed to remind him that art is nothing if not 'forensic'. Bhupen read out his stories such as 'Phoren Soap' and 'Maganbhai's Glue'. They were happy in this togetherness, which both knew meant nothing to them because it was unreal.

When Bhupen passed away in 2003, Mahasveta Devi did not cry. She said, 'Among your friends he was the only real one, all others are superficial.'

On a Sunday morning in January 2001, we were watching

the news on TV in Ahmedabad; suddenly we saw the newsreader abandon his desk and run out of the studio. In another couple of seconds, our own house in Baroda started shaking violently. We all ran out of the house shouting, 'It's an earthquake!' The great quake had hit Gujarat. The next day we drove through Ahmedabad. Everywhere there were collapsed and collapsing houses. She returned to Kolkata and started writing public appeals for help. For over a month she kept sending relief material.

The following year, Gujarat was struck by a greater, this time man-made, tragedy. The riots in Gujarat erupted on the last day of February. By 2 March, Mahasveta Devi had faxed a letter to the President asking for an inquiry by the CBI. In a week's time she was in Gujarat, when the cities were still under curfew. I will never forget the expression on her face when she spoke to the inmates of the Shah Alam relief camp. A Muslim woman who had seen eighteen members of her family, as well as relatives and neighbours killed before her eyes, was talking to Mahasveta Devi. I had to hold her as she fainted in anger and shock. She visited Gujarat twice during March and April 2002, speaking to small gatherings of peace-keepers and writers about the need for understanding, but I noticed that the idea of being in Gujarat no longer appealed to her. Her subsequent visits were mainly to spend a few quiet days with my wife Surekha and me.

Our days spent together have been very special for all three of us. When with us, Mahasveta Devi becomes our mother, friend and child, in turn. She narrates stories that we are unable to read, because they have yet to be translated into English. She speaks of her life and times, of experiences that she will be unable to include in the autobiography on which she has been working. She is with us as if she has always been with us, closer than a mother, sister or friend. It is difficult for me to believe that such a relationship can really exist. Yet, I know that she lives on a different plane, that Mahasveta Devi is not accessible to anyone.

Halfway through a perfectly normal breakfast, served after her medication, all of a sudden she exclaims, 'Ganesh—land—land is the root cause of it all. Give them land and everything will be "halright". Oh, this wretched "hestablishment".' As I pour another cup of black tea for her I ask, 'Do you remember our visit to that ex-minister's farmhouse?' She then tells Surekha how she saw women's undergarments of various fashion strewn in the toilet of the 'h-h-honourable ex-minister' when she was taken there by mistake by his attendants, and how 'mightily he frowned'. But even before we had finished laughing, she remarks in utmost pain, 'This woman's body is a curse!' Then she turns to me and remarks, 'You will not know, because you are not political.' The very next moment she is focussing on her cup of tea.

I have often wondered about the source of her strength, the literary influences that have shaped her powerful style of writing, the political philosophies that have gone into the making of her ideology. She confesses to having no influences, except that she mentions her uncle, the filmmaker Ritwik Ghatak, with a great sense of pride. I am often amazed at how someone like her, slated to be a middle-class housewife, has managed to transcend so many prisons to become what she is. What is the source of her remarkable memory, the frightening economy of her words, that great simplicity which, having distributed life between the necessary and the unnecessary, shuns all that is unnecessary? Is she an adivasi taken to literature, or a writer drawn to the adivasis?

Do I know Mahasveta Devi? Perhaps; perhaps not.

The Ascent of the Ordinary

Tarun J. Tejpal

In modern sport they have a phrase for it. It's called being 'in the zone'. Once or twice in a career, a gifted player arrives at a place inside his head where he can do no wrong. Intuition, judgement, hand-eye coordination—the very environment—fall into eloquent accord. Bad plays turn out good; luck takes up residence in the hip pocket; impossible moves become possible. The same player whose career was a question mark on 13 March 2001 at Eden Gardens—V.V.S. Laxman—becomes an exemplar, the definition of a kind of genius.

In 2004 when inscrutable India reasserted itself, Sonia Maino Gandhi—like Laxman stroking his way to an improbable 281—played the innings of her life. She began that year a journeyman politician, capable of a few things, incapable of much; less expected to deliver a miracle, more likely to preside over a debacle. Her chief perceived virtue a surname; her handicaps legion. As in the worst kind of army, even those who followed her into battle were convinced she would be bested. Crafty, effete Congressmen, whose only hope she was, displayed embarrassment in private: making cracks about her accent, feeling sorry for her innocence, lamenting their fate at being gifted this strange paradox of a leader whose surname was a sword but whose persona was straw.

What is the worth of the greatest weapon in the world without the arm that can wield it?

Worse, the battle she faced was by any standard daunting: a swaggeringly confident power-pumped ruling party—the BJP-led NDA—nimble in knotting alliances, capable of speaking in many voices, not handicapped by a need to adhere to any Queensberry rules, led, it believed, by a leader whose charismatic pull was not second to that of Jawaharlal Nehru and Indira Gandhi.

In sporting parlance, again, they would have said: no contest. And it is precisely what the Indian media said—its antennae snarled by psephologists and pret and stock markets and Johnny Walker pundits—precisely what the urban master-class pronounced. No contest. The advertisements for 'India Shining' blinding proprietor and writer alike. In the end they did the watchful lady in 10 Janpath a great favour, taking away from her the burden of victory, freeing her to strike forth as she chose. Only those who have been there know what a liberating thing it is to be a complete underdog. Those with nothing to lose sleep with open windows: opportunity, creativity, fresh air find easy ingress.

Sonia Gandhi began 2004 expected to achieve nothing; she ended it possessed of a stature that a former prime minister, Atal Behari Vajpayee, must well have envied. It was not tainted by a quest for personal power; it was not tainted by communalism; it was not tainted by the distressing penchant for saying one thing and doing another.

Exactly twenty years before Sonia's husband, Rajiv Gandhi, was ending the year similarly catapulted in stature. He had begun that year, 1984, as a nice—if callow—son of the prime minister. After a tumultuous year for the country—Operation Blue Star, Indira Gandhi's assassination, Bhopal—

the people had gifted him a historic mandate as he brought in them a surge of new hope. Everyone hoped he would turn us away from the growing cycle of divisive violence; a new dawn would break, regaining the reassurance of old decencies and the promise of modern ways. They placed in him more faith than they had in his imperious mother, and even in his singularly illustrious grandfather.

The true worth of that moment is still being debated. The calculus that will weigh the follies of political innocence—Shah Bano, Babri Masjid, Bofors—against the triumphs of visionary initiatives—new economy, new technology. History will take some more time to make its reckoning. In that light it is impossible to so early assess the meaning of 2004, to know if it will prove a watershed year in the political processes and directions of a new millennium India. But it is not impossible to assess Sonia Gandhi's place in it. If the year has lasting meaning, she will without doubt be its centrepiece.

What it's also possible to say is that compared to Rajiv, her achievement—though a mere third in terms of Lok Sabha seats won—is far greater. The Nehru-Gandhi was born to power, he had merely to stretch out his hand to receive it. In the life, education and ambition of the Italian girl there was nothing to prepare her for what has become her destiny.

Try to think of a parallel. A white woman in a brown land. Not Bhutan, not Nepal, not Sri Lanka. Not a land with finite borders and a finite people. But a land with infinite history, infinite culture, infinite numbers. A land of a thousand million people. A land with recent baggage of glorious anti-colonial struggle; a land continually rediscovering pride in its infinite innate worth. In such a land try and think of a white woman discovering an indigenous voice and finding in tens of millions an echo of it.

Try and find a parallel to Sonia Gandhi's triumph which unfurled breathlessly on Indian television screens in that magical May of 2004. Perhaps there is none.

Sonia Gandhi, many will wager with sound arguments, is not extraordinary. But what she pulled off in the year of her coming was more than extraordinary. It was miraculous. It was a triumph of many things. It told us many things. About ourselves. About her. About the nature of endeavour.

About ourselves, on the downside, it was yet another sad reminder that we are still a country of abject followers: believers in dynasties, feudalisms, the divine rights of rulers. We need a guiding hand; we need our destinies secure in the caress of paramount leaders.

On the flip side, the plus side, it told us we are a people of the greatest open embrace. Blessed with profound cultural securities, we are not easily threatened. We are never subsumed; we are never co-opted. In our body run a thousand cultural, linguistic and racial strains, acquired over millennia, each one making us more immune to the narrow fundamentalisms that have begun to challenge the world.

The town-criers, the masters of inquisition, may have got it wrong.

It is not we who have been co-opted by Sonia.

It is we who have co-opted her. Made her one of us.

She arrived here a pretty Italian girl; we have made her a stoic Indian woman. She arrived here with a European notion of the good life; we have imbued her with the oriental sense of a deeper purpose. She put her blood and sweat out on the line, and in totally unexpected fashion we gave her a mandate.

The fact is between leaders and followers there are the base adhesives of colour, creed, caste, religion, resume. But far, far more is built around hope, respect, belief and love. Sonia has already been tested on some of these; and she will continue to be again and again in the coming years. And it is only through continual reiterations of these that she will retain the space she has carved for herself in a forever fickle public mind.

By now it is fairly certain that we will never know what kind of prime minister and administrator she might have turned out. What we may get, over time, is an opportunity to evaluate what kind of nation-builder she was. And what we already know is that she has paid her dues. Democratic politics is always full of remarkable journeys. Hers could well be among the most remarkable of them all. More remarkable than those of Rajiv, Sanjay, Indira, Jawaharlal and Motilal; more remarkable than anything that will happen to Rahul and Priyanka. They were all born unto their destinies. Hers has been clawed out in the face of incalculable odds. In the ascent to Everest she was allowed to start from the final camp—from the Nehru-Gandhi household—but her legs were then tied and weights attached to them.

The story is familiar. Sonia Maino meets and loves Rajiv Gandhi in England and arrives in Delhi to marry him in the late sixties. Straight into the prime minister's house—nearly forty years ago—whereto India's satraps and chieftains lust forever to go. Loved of her mother-in-law, the redoubtable Indira Gandhi, she leads a life of happy domesticity amid the whirl of power politics and international visitors. She is good with menus, clothes, guests and, after the sudden death of young Sanjay Gandhi, lends a secretarial hand to her mother-in-law's arsenal of concerns. Living in India's most public family, she is a private presence—shadowy, retiring, elegant. Not accessible, not known, not arousing curiosity.

Easily the most unlikely candidate in that household to commandeer mass goodwill or power.

The immense—immense—challenge of India comes visiting on the 31st of October 1984 as Indira Gandhi is peppered with bullets by her bodyguards, and dies cradled in Sonia's arms. When her forty-year-old husband is anointed heir, she fights like a wildcat to protect the life she loves—of family intimacies and close friends. As her husband vaults into the public imagination, she remains who she has been—shadowy, retiring, elegant. There is the honeymoon of 414 Lok Sabha seats, the nightmare of Bofors, and the defeat of 1989. In failure, in adversity—as it always is—Rajiv Gandhi's true education has finally begun. There is unanimity that when he returns to power he will be refined of the hype, the naiveté, the cronyism. He will finally be the complete politician and leader he is meant to be.

On the night of 21 May 1991, in the middle of a new general election, the phone at 10 Janpath rings just short of 11 p.m. The immense—immense—challenge of India has come visiting again. Sonia Gandhi's wails fill the sprawling house. Hitherto the retainers have never heard a raised decibel. Someone is testing her most unfairly.

The next eight years are a mysterious ballet of Sonia's own anxieties and instincts, and the push and pull of Congress leaders desperate for the Nehru-Gandhi armour that gives them courage to do electoral battle. She maintains an uneasy peace with Narasimha Rao as he heads a Congress government, even as leaders queue up at 10 Janpath to importune her to seize the steering wheel of the party and keep it from careering off the road. Ever correct, she holds her fire. Does not intervene in party affairs, does not push appointments and people. In the public eye, she is still who she was: shadowy, inscrutable, the sphinx.

No one. Simply no one expects her to do anything

momentous, leave alone take over a creaking, careening Congress, slowly shearing off at the edges. Sonia heading the Congress is a conceit: it is not meant to be a reality. It is an idea that is meant to allow other ideas to come into play—such as the advent of Rahul and Priyanka: it is not meant to be a reality. No one believes she has the panoply of skills needed to lead an Indian political party—cunning, camaraderie, casteism, compromise, corruption, charisma.

She is an idea meant to allow other ideas to come into play.

She is not meant to become the idea herself.

The surreal coronation of the wheedling Sitaram Kesari as Congress president, the howls for help from old party hands and loyalists—among them Arjun Singh, R.K. Dhawan, Ambika Soni, Ahmed Patel, Suresh Pachauri, Digvijay Singh—and some indefinable impulse (to which she herself has alluded often) to rescue the fraying Nehruvian vision—the idea of India, liberal, secular, modern—all of it finally forces her hand.

She takes over the party, an unlikely helmsman. Surrounded by sycophants, working every day on her Hindi, trying hard to divine the byzantine code of a party of unparalleled size and disarray, she has her work fairly cut out, till someone decides to test her a little more. There is an unexpected rebellion in 1999 as Sharad Pawar, Purno Sangma and Tariq Anwar raise the very same bogey her Sangh Parivar opponents have been waving: her foreign origins. This is a crippling blow, the one moment she wants to throw in the towel, retreat into her shell of quiet aesthetics, genteel books and family intimacies. Once again the Congress trenches vomit out importuners and pleaders—so relentlessly and apparently so sincerely that she is forced to reconsider.

In hindsight the revolt was good for her. The vaccine that fixed the disease. She came back much stronger, her party now a poodle on a leash. But fixing the party was only one part of her challenge. The mighty one was to take on the shouting armies of the Sangh Parivar who were buoyed by power and convinced they could undo her in a hundred ways, from her foreign origins to her accented Hindi to her inability to be the backslapping politician who rules India's voteways. For three years, relentlessly, a torrent of calumny was thrown her way; there were continual attempts to humiliate her for her language, her origins, her lack of political savvy, her ostensible avarice and dynastic politics.

Enough trash to have despaired the most stout.

Clearly she had to dig deep within herself to stand her ground. Clearly some memory of lessons learnt in the shadows of Indira and Rajiv—in the very womb of pulsing power—stirred. Most important of all—and it is clear in her every action—she learnt to go beyond the line of fear. Fear of insult, fear of rejection, fear of failure, fear of persecution. All these had stared her in the face every day since she entered politics, an alien animal in a hostile jungle. There had been triumphs—states won—and there had been failures—states lost; there had been resolutions—to go it alone; to adopt moral and legal funding—and there had been compromises—with Laloo and Mulayam and the stigmatized candidates of the anti-Sikh riots. But clearly there had been less and less fear.

And it is this—less and less fear—that finally brought her to the summit of Everest.

It is when she learnt the art of the open embrace, when she became unafraid of the open embrace—with other parties, with people—that the world began to shift. The most valuable lesson she remembered was that of her mother-in-law. Indira

Gandhi was always clear. Don't worry about the 150 chatterers of Delhi. When you want what you want, go to the people. Only they can give it to you, not those who talk in Delhi.

In the beginning of 2004, before anyone had even put their feet on the starting blocks, Sonia Gandhi did just that. She turned her back on the cynics and the critics and with a display of unsuspected energy and resolve—before the election bugles had been sounded—sailed into the arms of the people, from western Uttar Pradesh to every nook and corner of the subcontinent.

She smiled, she waved, she shook hands, she hugged, and miraculously a moribund Congress—battered into a defeatist mindset by the NDA's bellowing tellytalkers—began to find its feet. Even so observers wondered why the rest of the party was doing so little, and she so much. The abiding and greatest irony of the fourteenth general elections will remain that the most tireless warrior for the cause of Indian secularism and liberalism was the one they kept denouncing as a foreigner. That sixty years after Independence the chief keeper of the idea of India was a non-Indian.

Though the story of the general elections of 2004 is Sonia Gandhi, the story of Sonia Gandhi's true triumph actually begins after the victory at the hustings.

The curious thing about history is how often it turns on the ordinary gesture. The writing of an article. The making of a speech. Ejection from a train. Incarceration in an island prison. An election. A resignation. The acceptance of a post. The rejection of a post.

Ernest Hemingway—with his penchant for the *bon mot*— once said, 'In life it doesn't matter where you come from; all that matters is where you go.' It is a mantra all strugglers hold close as they soldier against the fiends of privilege and prejudice. It is a variant on the principle of you are what you do. It lays down that the final playing field of men should have no fences of race, caste, colour, creed.

It is the utopia against which we mostly fail. And occasionally succeed. Sonia Gandhi may have come from Orbassano in Italy—or wherever Subramaniam Swamy thinks she actually comes from—but in that dramatic May of 2004 where she went was to the very top of the Indian political heap. Having held together a Congress that was beginning to come apart like an ungummed book; having survived enough insults to have flayed a rhino's skin; having won an election in which no one gave her a ghost of a chance; having got the assent of every secular party to her candidature; having arrived where nothing more stood between her and the post of the prime minister; having got where every Indian politician would die to go, she put herself in between.

In that hot, heady midsummer month, her partymen predictably made much theatre trying to remove her from the way so she could wear the crown. In time-honoured Congress tradition the high-tent of sycophancy went up swiftly and the circus was unleashed. Mawkish speeches were made, guns pulled, trees climbed, roads slept on, tears shed. But she stood her ground.

Orchestrated or unorchestrated, that rejection is now universally recognized as a masterstroke.

Having already gone from ordinary to extraordinary in the course of a long election, she had now in one unexpected act become historic.

Sushma Swaraj could keep her hair. Uma Bharti, her bile. Govindacharya, his nasal harangues. Venkaiah Naidu, his doggerel. L.K. Advani, the yatras. Vajpayee, his dithering.

Manmohan Singh, the crown. Congress, the power.

And she?

And she a moral lustre not seen in Indian political life for a long time.

Even now, so much later, speculation has not settled on why she did not seize the laurel. Many say she never intended to. But then why the charade? The unanimous election by the Congress Parliamentary Party. The meetings with the allies. The letters of support from them. The tryst with the President. Was it only to prove the point (and who can fault that, given the history of abuse directed at her) that she could win it, have it for the taking, and then turn it down? Others feel the gathering hysteria of Sushma-Uma-Govindacharya and suchlike hell-raisers unnerved her, made her fear she would risk losing the battle even in the moment of winning it. One school spoke of security threats, and her children's apprehensions. And another—issuing from the ever-cranking mills of the Hindu right wing—declared that the President had warned her there was legal trouble in store if she chose to become the prime minister. Papers published it as the gospel, and Rashtrapati Bhawan was forced to issue a denial.

Even if all the above reasons were in play, it must have been a monumentally difficult decision. Anyone who skirts the fringes of power is aware of its immense seductions. None can resist its ride. Those who don't have it, crave it intemperately; those who have it, are terrified of losing it. This fear—of losing it—is what made Atal Behari Vajpayee a smaller man than he is. In his election rallies he attacked his opponents for possessing *satta ka lobh*, but failed the test each time the same question was posed of him. He allowed his government to mercilessly destroy *Tehelka* even though he knew we were clean and only doing our job.

He found a few vaguely ameliorative words during the carnage of Gujarat, but could find neither his conscience nor the will to act.

You are what you do. Not what you say. Not what you mean.

Gujarat could have made Vajpayee great, levitated him beyond his peers. But it left him a small man. Indians tend to believe morality is a slippery eel that can assume any shape and wriggle past anything. We also tend to feel that if things are left alone they will sort themselves out. But great leadership is about the act of moral faith. About imposing a superior will upon the dross of the everyday. It is about lifting the levels of public discourse and conduct so we are all forced to become more than what we are.

But too many governments in too many decades have worked at making us less than who we are.

Gujarat could have made Vajpayee great. By the ordinary act. Of a resignation.

Sonia was made great by an ordinary act. Of a rejection.

Somehow, she managed to look through the fog of power to see that her ascension could create one more fissure in a land increasingly disfigured by cuts and slashes. She could see what she could achieve by becoming the prime minister. But miraculously she also saw how much more she could pull off by not becoming the prime minister.

She saw the moral answer buried in the riddle of power.

He has most power who craves least power.

In the surprising turnaround year of 2004 what she did was to remind us once again of the immense potency of the moral act. Make no mistake, morality is still the greatest strategy in politics and public life. The very smart boys of the political backrooms—crunching numbers, cutting deals—

imagine that the winning of votes and public approval is just a matter of computers, money, hype, and tactics. It is not.

Leadership is first and last a moral act. Its morality is its unstoppable strategy.

It is why Indians venerate the *rishi* over the *rajan*.

It is why the greatest Indian of them all never held a formal post.

Often, Sonia says that she looks to deliver the vision of Indira and Rajiv. That is where she may be wrong. The vision that she has to work to deliver is still the liberal-humanist-secular one of Jawaharlal, in every way leagues ahead of those who have followed.

For Jawaharlal, and his mentor Mohandas, every public act was a moral one.

And it is only intuitive knowledge of this that has brought Sonia so far.

No matter her reasons for doing so, Sonia managed to achieve many things by refusing to become prime minister. She completely defanged a divisive and inflammatory issue—a foreign-born as prime minister—and put a poultice on every abraded emotion. She placed a fine man in the prime ministerial chair: for Indians there can only be great pride in knowing that the man at the helm of the nation is utterly honest and efficient. And she has re-established the distinction—after decades—between the head of the party and the head of the government. In the early days there were those who carped that the arrangement works best when the prime minister is stronger than the party chief, but to be fair, two years on, there is no evidence yet to back such a claim. In fact, both party and government may have benefited from the division.

In the middle of 2004, she left the BJP in a place of some

distress. She showed them up in poor light—their invective, their posturing, their arrogance, their stance of the sullen loser. She put the Congress in a very sweet place. In the warmth of her moral halo. And herself in an unassailable position: she who wanted power, but not for herself.

She may not have expanded her moral lustre in the years the UPA has been in power, but somehow she has managed to not dilute it either. Once again her old virtues have served her well: caution, reticence, correctness. With a finely calibrated refinement, she has avoided the vulgarities—governmental interference and bungling, deal-making, public preening— that instantly afflict those in power. With shrewd political instinct, trying to stay close to the people, she has used every opportunity to share public distress wherever it breaks in the country. Most of her photo-ops have been of her arriving in a calamity zone, before anyone else. And, unexpectedly, she has allowed Manmohan Singh to become his own man— confident captain of his ship, even if not its proprietor.

Two years after the famous victory she may no longer be in the zone, but her instincts are still working beautifully. She pulled the plug out of the clamorous mike of the Opposition's campaign on the office-of-profit issue by the simple act—once more—of a resignation. Suddenly the opposition uproar was gone, and all you could hear was the mewling of the sycophantic hordes of the Congress. Once again she had deployed a weapon Indian politicians have forgotten to use, the moral move. The answer to the riddle of power—he has most who craves least.

With success, with moral lustre, with power, has also come a greater ease. Now she is willing to bend low to listen to anyone—look at her relations with her allies—because she has grown so tall. The roller-coaster of power, exile, calumny, power has also gifted her a fine admixture of shrewdness and wisdom. She can walk the tightrope of power—giving her prime minister his full due, steering clear of an overt presence in government, even as she keeps an eagle eye on all that is happening, ensuring her pack doesn't begin to hunt each other.

In some ways this is a triumph not of genius but of the uncluttered mind. Stick to the fundamentals, recognize the line between right and wrong, don't overcalculate, and things will be fine.

Keep it simple.

Do what is right and seemly, and it will be seen to be right and seemly.

Outstanding leaders are not terribly clever people.

Outstanding leaders have rock solid fundamentals.

The more moral the fundamentals are, the more magnetic is the appeal of the leader. Two years is too little to reach a conclusion but Sonia's rare gesture of renunciation, the advent of the good Dr Manmohan Singh, and the right noises about social justice, development and economic progress may well herald some return of morality to public life. She has also put the monkey on the backs of her partymen and her allies, calling them all to a higher order of conduct. They have to watch their pettiness; and also be aware that the voter—now possessed of a new gauge of assessment—will judge their excesses and tantrums harshly.

It would be absurd to imagine that in all this we have already begun to reclaim the politics of decency, or that Sonia has dazzled us with astute and visionary moves. In fact the disappointments have been many too: the appointment and continuation of old Congress politicians who are both corrupt and dinosaurs; the utter missingness of the young in the new government (leading to whispers that she will not allow anyone to upstage her son); enough dubious moments from Volcker to Quattrochi; the absence of radical initiatives, creative responses to the chronic problems of the *aam admi*.

The disappointments may have more to do with our expectations of her than her real performance. For a long time we thought she was capable of nothing; and then suddenly post the May of 2004 we thought she could do it all. The fact is her administrative-intellectual-political abilities can only accrete slowly, and the challenges of India are not to be sorted in a day or by a person, no matter a Nehru-Gandhi or a Mahatma.

Everything in life has to be judged in the context of its potential. What was the material and what was made out of it? You cannot build a brick wall out of bamboo. That is one way to look at Sonia. Assess the material, assess the magic. Italian doll, Indian devi.

Look at her today. She glows, she smiles, she speaks with easy confidence. She not only won an impossible victory for her ragtag party, but continues to find grace in the time of her triumph. She is a prime example of the transformative life, the ordinary life made extraordinary through the acceptance of challenge. If she stays the path she could end up catalyzing incredible things, unencumbered as she is by the baggage of caste, community, clan.

Many questions, however, still persist.

Does she now have native instinct?

Of course she never will, but that only makes her work harder.

Does she mean well? Does she have fortitude? Can she lead her party? Do the people back her? Has she earned our respect?

Yes. Yes. Yes.

Is she now an Indian?

As much as a foreign-born can ever be.

And she is ratified by the scriptures, which are clear. Action is all. You are what you do.

Interestingly, above all, she has been that most Indian of beings, a good *karmayogi*. Her triumph is a lesson in the virtue of endeavour. The splendour of action. Better still, as the scriptures tell us, detached action. She continues to give evidence of that too. There is a zone of calm from where she operates (with her personal avengers, Priyanka and Rahul, close in her orbit). She is known to often admit that she knows her life is ever on the line. But the anxiety does not seem to mark her conduct.

Will she go down in history as a great and visionary leader?

Probably not. And yet you can never tell. She still wears a tangled crown, power without power. But then you don't have to be an elephant, you just have to be an exemplary mahout. In that her record is reasonable, because she is a learner. From the NDA she has learnt the art of coalitions, from her mother-in-law the art of campaigning, and from India the art of the open embrace. That odd exasperating trait of many great leaders—the art of enigma, which sates and teases followers in equal measure—she of course has a patent on.

Her critics say she is insecure and holds power close to herself; her supporters say Congress leaders would fall upon each other if she slackened the reins.

Her critics say she wants Rahul and Priyanka to inherit the earth; her supporters say it is Congress leaders who do not leave them alone, for the children are their next ticket to the people and power.

Her critics say a fawning Congress is thrusting greatness upon her; her supporters say she alone among the last generation of Nehru-Gandhis has gained it with her singular efforts.

Her critics say that basically she is very ordinary. That may well be. But what Sonia Gandhi has pulled off in her storybook life is more than extraordinary. It is a miracle. We can be sure even if she never does another thing of note ever, the year of 2004 will always belong to her, as will the unique space she has carved out for herself in the maelstrom of Indian politics and public life.

Looking for Indira Gandhi

Sunil Khilnani

The glassy memorial that stands in the garden where Indira Gandhi was assassinated by her own bodyguards in 1984 is among the most visited secular sites in India. Morning and afternoon, busloads of Indians arrive from across the country—families, young and old, stream through the grounds, noisy but respectful.

Though more than twenty years dead, Mrs Gandhi stays vivid in popular memory—to most Indians she is the best prime minister they have ever had. She dominated India's public life from the mid-1960s to the mid-1980s: with the sole exception of her father, Jawaharlal Nehru, no other Indian has put so deep an impress on their country's independent life.

But she is a bogey to India's present-day political and intellectual classes. The Hindu chauvinist-led coalition government, till recently in power, contained several members who were imprisoned by her during the Emergency (the period between 1975 and 1977 when she suspended democratic liberties), while the Left and liberal intelligentsia blame her for India's current travails—corruption and nepotism, a until recently retarded economy, fraying secularism. Writers too have stitched her up—from V.S. Naipaul to Salman Rushdie, she lives in the literary imagination as a malevolent, megalomaniac leader who ended the innocence of Nehru's post-independence idyll, and was responsible for—in Rushdie's phrase—'the smashing, the pulverizing, the irreversible discombobulation of the children of midnight'.

Mrs Gandhi is independent India's most puzzling politician. Enigmatic and often opaque in person, her political persona is also hard to fix on. In power, she seemed a woman of supreme self-assurance, exuding a haughty *froideur*; but in private, she spoke of self-doubt and diffidence—'I was so sure I had nothing in me to be admired,' she confided to one of her close friends days before her death. She never conformed to any one of the supposed 'idioms' of Indian politics—the saintly, traditional or the modern—but moved adeptly between them. (Much of her success derived from her recognition of the historically dislocated character of India's politics, its existence as a collision field for different historical time-lines.)

She was the daughter of a politician who wore his principles on his sleeve, but herself seemed to personify a ruthless instinct for political survival. What, if anything at all, did she actually stand for? It is difficult too, to judge her own responsibility for the drift on Indian politics. Was she the instigator of a coarser, more clamorous, fragmented society, or was she simply a mirror, reflecting what was already underway?

What is now clear is the deeply paradoxical nature of her legacy. During her lifetime, she appeared invariably as the greatest threat to democracy in India, and certainly she weakened the constitutional regularities that her father had tried to establish. Yet the enduring historical effect of her rule was to throw open the state to popular demands, to make it accessible to new groups, and to make Indian society still more political. She branded a certain idea of democracy on the Indian political imagination. She made democracy ordinary—not pretty, just ordinary—and the thousands of Indians who file past her memorial know that.

Indira Nehru Gandhi was born in November 1917, the only child of Jawaharlal and Kamala Nehru. The Nehru house in Allahabad—Anand Bhawan—was established by Jawaharlal's father, Motilal Nehru, a formidably ambitious lawyer of Kashmiri ancestry. Indira's early years coincided with the house becoming the epicentre of the Congress-led national movement that opposed British rule, and she was raised in a relentlessly political household. The family itself was an untypical one: across several generations, the Nehrus helped to invent an idea of the modern Indian family—one which moved away from the Hindu 'joint family' and towards a more internally spacious model, where deliberation and personal choice were (within significant limits) encouraged, and where women were expected to take an active role. As a family, the Nehrus were able to find a novel way to connect the private world to the new professional world of politics.

The story of Indira's own life is one of making herself a full member of this political family. Being a Nehru meant becoming a political being, to an extent where she could say, in an interview to the *New York Times* a few weeks after becoming prime minister in 1966, that 'politics is the centre of everything'. She might have been enunciating the family motto, and she was to discover that living up to it could be a strenuous and painful business. Linked to and sustaining that sense of politics as lying at the centre of everything was a belief, shared by all the Nehrus, in historical destiny, in an assigned role on the stage of history. Nehru himself was steeped in this historical self-regard—he perpetually invested his personal life with historical significance, and the rooms and corridors of Anand Bhawan must often have felt like a live tableaux of India's present and future history, with Mahatma Gandhi, Annie Besant, Sardar Patel, all crowding its hallways (it is indeed today home to a museum).

But the Nehru household was also marked by disruption, and could often be eerily vacant. Indira's parents, aunts, relatives, family friends, all went in and out of prison, at the Raj's pleasure. Her mother Kamala, when out of jail, was confined by illness and often in hospital. In the absence of adults, Indira found herself in charge and having to run things from an early age. Her upbringing amidst this debris of familial life invites psychological speculation about her loneliness, insecurities, fears, and a certain mythic portraiture of Indira's youth has emerged—the distant father, the spiteful aunt, the invalid mother. A youthful acquaintance of hers, Urmila Haksar, remembered how 'everyone used to refer to her, though not within her hearing, as "poor Indu", "poor Kamala's child", "what a sad life, poor girl has had".' [sic]

Her youthful relationships were rarely direct or proximate, but were splayed by distances. We know most about her bond with her father. Nehru, himself often confined within those great British institutions of self-improvement—public school, Cambridge, His Majesty's prisons—developed a talent which made him probably the greatest Indian letter writer of the twentieth century (certainly the greatest in the English language). His first book, a sweeping survey of world history in which he tried to adopt a non-European perspective, was written as letters to his daughter while he was in prison—a nationalist variant of the Victorian father's advice-book to his daughter.

During the last decade of her life, Kamala suffered from tuberculosis. In age mother and daughter were only seventeen years apart (they were often mistaken for sisters). But her illness made her seem like an older invalid, and she rarely had the energy or forcefulness of a young mother. Kamala came from a background worlds apart from the Nehrus, and her life was blighted too by the tortuous effort involved in becoming a Nehru—the strain broke her health, and cracked her confidence. Indira witnessed this happening, and came to detest the way her mother was treated by the family—especially by Nehru's two younger sisters, Vijayalakshmi Pandit and Krishna Hutheesingh.

Illness was a difficult condition in the Nehru household: Nehru preened himself over his own fitness, and regarded illness almost as a moral failing, an abnegation of duties. The letters between husband and wife rarely strayed from discussions of health, to the point where an exasperated Nehru once wrote to Kamala that 'there is a kind of sameness about you and illness.' Indira, herself frail, outwardly diffident, given to silent moods, and often in indifferent health, accompanied and nursed Kamala through much of her final illness.

It was the memory of her mother's isolation and physical decline that led Indira to the man she finally married, in what appears to have been a classic compensatory act. In her last years, Kamala had befriended and taken comfort in the attentions of a young man, a Parsi of lowly background and somewhat obscure pedigree, named Feroze Gandhy (the Parsi spelling was later amended, at Nehru's suggestion, to blur his different belonging). He was a bold and in some ways engaging young man: swept up in the excitement of nationalist agitation, he was given to impulsive and romantic escapades. Nehru never liked his barrack-room style and when, just a couple of years after Kamala's death, he learned from his daughter—then in England and studying at Oxford—of her desire to marry Feroze (in London at the time), Nehru did all he could to dissuade her.

Indira was now herself ill with tuberculosis, and Nehru used the argument of medical treatment to separate the two by bringing her back to India, in the hope that her head if not her heart might cool. The correspondence between father and daughter from these years radiates a searing, convulsive quality: it reveals a relationship that, in the wake of Kamala's death, took on a frightening intensity, charged with accusation and guilt, with anger and a deep emotional interdependence. After this period the two never again communicated so rawly and openly—things become unspoken and subterranean.

For a few years, Indira tried not to be a Nehru. She defied her father, married Feroze in 1942, and aspired to create her own domestic life. She and Feroze set up home, had two sons—Rajiv in 1944, Sanjay in 1946—and Feroze tried his hand at a career as a journalist (working for his father-in-law's newspaper: Nehru was less than impressed, urging his daughter to edit Feroze's 'Biblical English', and curb his excessive use of 'verily'). But Feroze's earnings were erratic, and as a family the newly married Gandhis depended on money from Nehru. The marriage was also uneasy: Feroze was easily distracted by his roving eye, and in 1946 Indira decided to move back with her boys to live with Nehru, now effectively the head of the Indian government in New Delhi.

The maws of politics were closing in around her. At India's independence in 1947, Nehru, now Prime Minister, was living in the grand former residence of the British Commander-in-Chief: Indira took over the management of the household, and stepped into the role of her father's social hostess. She came into contact with Indian and international leaders, and during the 1950s underwent a slow self-transformation into a political being—the decade brought a crucial metamorphosis in her life.

Indira began to accompany her father on official visits (she travelled overseas two dozen times between 1949 and 1959, including to the famous Bandung Conference in 1955, where she exercised a calming influence on her father's spleen), and from this time on there were constant nudges to her from within the Congress Party to stand for parliament. She resisted these, but did enter more deeply into internal party matters (a subject in which Nehru had little interest), and began to move up the hierarchy of the Congress Party.

Her father was scrupulous in not involving her in political matters—he saw her more 'as an assistant than a confidante or adviser'. She too at this stage seemed restrained in her ambitions. As she wrote to her father in 1953, 'I do want to reorganize my life and get out of all the silly committees. I am so sick of people doing social work as a step up the political and social set [sic] ladder, and equally sick of all the vague goodness of the so-called Gandhians.' But that same year she made a visit to the USSR and this seemed to boost her, giving her for the first time a sense of her own independent power. She began to offer unsolicited advice to her father about appointments and other matters—often put up to it by Nehru's manipulative private secretary, M.O. Mathai.

The Nehrus are not only India's most political family: to many they are also its ruling family, a modern 'dynasty' rivalled only by the Kennedys, and like them enveloped in myth and tragedy. That successive generations could have possessed such power in a democracy naturally raises questions: one of the most persistent is whether Nehru intended his daughter to succeed him, and schemed to this end. The short answer is no. It was a series of chance events that took her into the prime minister's office.

In September 1960 Feroze died suddenly of a heart attack. Despite their strained relations, his death affected Indira deeply, and further reinforced her desire for a domestic life away from politics (she even thought of moving to the English countryside). It seems also to have affected her younger son, Sanjay, in ways that left Indira prey to his manipulation. Pupul Jayakar, a friend and earlier biographer of Indira Gandhi, noted that Feroze's death left Sanjay 'bereft and resentful of his mother whom he held responsible for the neglect and death of his father'. Sanjay Gandhi had fastened on his mother's weakest spot (after all, she had herself accused her own father of exactly this neglect) and he was to play on this in later years to disastrous effect. Mrs Gandhi's thin skin on this matter can be gathered from the fact that, when years later Salman Rushdie repeated the story about her neglect of Feroze, she sued Rushdie for libel.

Her own father, meanwhile, was becoming increasingly dependent on her. Nehru was broken mentally and physically by India's defeat at the hands of China in their 1962 war, and his failing health meant that more responsibilities were put upon her. Yet, rather than seizing this as an opportunity to thrust herself forward, she seemed to shrink from the political spotlight.

Nehru died in May 1964. He had named no successor but had indicated his preference for a man named Lal Bahadur Shastri, who duly took over. Loyal, soft-spoken, courteous, Shastri considered it right manners to take in his mentor's daughter and offered Indira Gandhi a post in his Cabinet, the relatively unimportant portfolio of Information and Broadcasting. She accepted: partly out of a sense of duty, fulfilling her identity as a Nehru that previously she had tried to escape, and partly because she needed the income. She had no financial resources or inherited wealth, apart from the royalties from Nehru's books; the family house, Anand Bhawan, had been donated to the nation as a museum, and she could no longer live in the prime minister's residence; Feroze had not left her any property.

Barely two years in office, Shastri himself died in January 1966, having just concluded the Tashkent Treaty that ended the 1965 war with Pakistan. Faced with this unexpected succession crisis, senior Congress leaders were in confusion. They now turned to Mrs Gandhi, but not because she promised to be a great leader in the line of her father—on the contrary, they fixed on her exactly because she seemed to personify antithetical qualities. It was her evident unsuitability that attracted them to her. She was without any power base in the party or country; female, a poor speaker, with no articulated political vision or ideological passion, she seemed a soft touch. How wrong they were. Once in office, power seemed to unleash a hormonal rush in her—aged almost fifty, she was rejuvenated. The desultoriness of her earlier years was shaken off, and her life acquired a new keenness, as she discovered an appetite for power.

Her premiership opened with a flourish. A couple of months after taking office, she made her first overseas visit as prime minister to the United States. She took Washington and New York by storm: according to Robert Komer, she 'vamped' Lyndon Johnson, and Johnson was moved to declare that he wanted to make sure 'no harm comes to this girl'. He promised $9 million in aid to India; she, in return, offered understanding on the American adventure in Vietnam.

Relations between the two countries seemed set to blossom, in contrast to the general chill surrounding them during her father's lifetime.

But, while she seemed to thrive personally, the broader situation facing her party and country was glum. Economic crisis—brought on by two wars and successive monsoon failures—forced her into moves that backfired. A condition of US aid had been a devaluation of the Indian currency: her announcement of a crashing 60 per cent devaluation of the rupee was, however, met with unanimous criticism in India. It seemed to confirm the old fears—that had fed the national movement—about India's vulnerability to international pressures, and built what ultimately grew into a paranoia about national sovereignty. The reactions to her move left a deep stain on her own economic thinking: it convinced her to stick with protectionist measures, to adopt populist policies, and to mistrust dependence on foreign assistance, however smilingly it might appear to be proffered.

In 1967 she had to face her first general election as prime minister; it was also the first time she had had to contest a parliamentary seat. She won her own seat with a huge majority, but the Congress Party turned in its worst performance ever, losing control of eight of India's regional states (including the most populous ones), and it was left with a small parliamentary majority. Indira Gandhi seized this as an opportunity to strengthen her own position. Catching the party at its weakest, she remade it: she split it, changed its internal character, and pulled it leftwards. The Congress Party was the great historic symbol of national unity, functioning as a capacious umbrella-like structure. Its strong central command had always given a long leash to the leaders from the regional states, relying on the provincial 'bosses' to tend clients, and to deliver support and votes in return for benefits negotiated from the centre.

Mrs Gandhi saw a need to break herself free from the grip of the old regional leaders who had put her in power. She sidelined them in two ways. After splitting the party—something that would have been unthinkable for her father—she changed the object of loyalty, from the party itself and its local leaders, to her own person. She did this by altering the forms of party finance. Previously such matters had been kept away from the central leadership. Nehru, prim about mechanics, had left the vulgar business of graft to his regional bosses—they hustled money from supporters and used this for electioneering in their own patches. Indira Gandhi abolished this system: henceforth, cash was delivered straight to her private secretaries—bypassing the regional bosses—and the distribution of election expenses to candidates was controlled directly from her office. The rupees came first in briefcases, then in suitcases—through this 'suitcase politics' she was able to create a material chain of loyalty between her chosen party men and herself.

She also set out to establish a direct relation with the electorate, again bypassing the party and its seasoned leaders. This she did by shifting her rhetoric to the Left, inventing a magical radicalism. Banks were nationalized, the princely families divested of privileges they had been constitutionally promised, and an electoral slogan at once supremely simple and blissfully hazy was devised: '*Garibi Hatao*' or 'Remove Poverty' (as she confessed to a journalist, she spoke socialism because that was what the people wanted to hear). In 1971 she called a snap election, ran a personalized campaign that projected herself as the sole issue at stake—as the unique scourge of poverty—and appealed directly to the poorest and lowest in the social order, to India's outcastes, Muslims, women. She achieved a landslide majority.

On top at home, international triumph now followed. The military leadership of West Pakistan was at this time pursuing a genocidal policy against the Bengalis of East Pakistan, and thousands of refugees were flowing into India. There was universal international condemnation, except from the US government, which sided with Pakistan: a product of the game of Chinese cat's-cradle being played by Nixon and Kissinger. It became apparent to Mrs Gandhi that military action against Pakistan was inevitable; she was given cause when a trigger-happy General Yahya Khan, the Pakistani leader, launched an attack on India in December 1971. The war was short, and a total victory for Mrs Gandhi. Her nerve and decisiveness during the campaign was formidable.

In five fast years, she had been transformed: in 1966 old colleagues of her father had referred to her as a 'dumb doll', a 'chit of a girl'. Now, at the peak of her career, she was named the most admired woman in the world by an American Gallup poll, had become one of the very few non-western leaders accorded respect in the citadels of world power, and seemed to her own people to have acquired semi-divine powers.

She used her new power to strike a deal with Pakistan at the ensuing peace summit held at Simla. Over the perennial thorn of Kashmir, she established with her counterpart Zulfikar Ali Bhutto an informal agreement to observe as the de facto border between the two countries the Line of Control (this was the ceasefire line established after the Pakistan-instigated invasion of Kashmir in 1948). She followed this two years later by announcing that India had conducted a nuclear test explosion for, as she described it, 'peaceful purposes'. It was a coy admission of India's nuclear abilities, which in time developed into an effective 'nuclear option' strategy. Her own role in deciding to take India down the nuclear path remains as ambiguous as her larger strategy: according to a leading historian of India's nuclear programme, in the secret debate leading up to the decision, 'she listened . . . and said, "Let's have it".'

In India's domestic politics, though, her political career was unfolding in democratic hubris. She had become so sure of her legitimacy, based on her electoral endorsement, that she convinced herself of the dispensability of constitutional constraints and procedures over the exercise of power. She had embraced a Jacobin conception of political power, an unfiltered view of democracy as direct and popular. Her acts had altered the meaning of democracy in the popular imagination—reducing it to signify quite simply the winning of power through elections, neglecting altogether the sense in which it was also a way of regulating the exercise of power. This demotic sense spread over the Indian political imagination, both elite and popular.

She centralized power, draining it away from the regional state governments and channelling it towards New Delhi. With the old arenas of debate and decision within the party eliminated, she surrounded herself with a group of highly intelligent and sophisticated men, leftist and technocratic in bent, and most of Kashmiri origin: P.N. Haksar, D.P. Dhar, P.N. Dhar, T.N. Kaul. Simultaneously, her younger son, Sanjay, was now elbowing his way onto the political stage. An ambitious gadfly with a marked capacity to attract distasteful young men on the make, after various abortive efforts to establish himself as the Indian Henry Ford by developing a cheap 'people's car' (he had trained, rather ineffectually, at the Rolls Royce works as a teenager), he plumped for a political career. He established a 'Youth Congress', a thuggish motley of scented young men with bad shoes, ruthless in their methods. This now began to fill the vacuum in the party created by Mrs Gandhi's destruction of its organization and old leadership.

Indira Gandhi's centralization and legislative free-handedness—she appealed to her parliamentary majorities to introduce sweeping legislative changes and constitutional amendments—provoked two waves of dissent, whose consequences still reverberate: the first resulted in the Emergency, the second in her own assassination. In 1974-75, severe economic conditions sparked a series of agitations in the west and east of the country, as well as a nationwide railway strike; in June 1975, a court judgement overturned Mrs Gandhi's election to parliament on the basis of a tiny infringement of electoral procedure. She became convinced that there was a large-scale conspiracy to overthrow her, possibly with international backing (a not entirely deluded hunch: Salvador Allende had been deposed shortly before, Mujibur Rahman was assassinated shortly after, both with the involvement of the CIA). Confronted with having to resign as prime minister, she decided to declare an Emergency, drawing upon state powers inherited intact from the Raj.

The Emergency lasted till 1977. Its history is extremely difficult to write, given the absence of definitive sources, the number of conflicting memories and views, and a generalized self-induced Alzheimer's condition among all who played a role in its events.

Although the powers absorbed by the government in the wake of the Emergency's declaration were sweeping, and seemed to be the prelude to an era of authoritarian rebuilding, in fact very little was actually done. There was plenty of concentrated nastiness, in which Sanjay Gandhi and his acquaintances played a leading role: the press was muzzled, political dissenters and opponents imprisoned, sterilizations were enforced, slums were razed in the name of 'city beautiful' schemes. But no major social or economic reforms were set in motion, nor even any Ceaucescuan mausoleums built; the main victim was the Constitution, and the liberal compass of India's democratic life.

Explanations of the Emergency tend to veer between labelling it the product of the biographical quirks of mother and son, and seeing it as a lapse of Indian society back in its cultural fate: dynasticism, despotism, and other oriental vices. In fact, it was neither. It was a critical episode in the history of the conflict between the two ideas—the state, and democracy—that have defined modern India's history. The Emergency is best seen as a parodic rendition of desire to return the Indian state to the hands of a Platonic do-good elite—at the very time when (as a result of Mrs Gandhi's own electoral style) the democratic idea was achieving an unprecedented diffusion across Indian society.

In effect, she was stepping on the brake pedal and accelerator at the same time. By suppressing democratic freedoms, Mrs Gandhi hoped to de-politicize India, and to entrust political decisions to a supposedly benevolent technocratic elite, to a 'committed' bureaucracy and judiciary. In fact, the effects were opposite, and succeeded in politicizing India still more profoundly. Deprived of their rights, people began to sense just how significant these might be. When she called elections in 1977, they exercised their rights resoundingly and voted out her and her party.

By 1980, though, she was back in power. The new government that had hoped to replace her—a ragtag of the disgruntled, the unprincipled, and the merely hopeful—collapsed in internal bickering. Within a few months of her return to power, Sanjay Gandhi was killed in a plane crash while performing acrobatics over the capital. It marked the beginning of her final, catastrophic phase in power. She had now to face the dissent provoked by her centralizing urges, and by the breakdown of structures that might have moderated these forms of dissent. Across the country, regionalist movements—always a potential form of political protest in India—escalated their demands and actions: some actually pressed for secession, all were prepared to use violence. In Punjab to the west, Assam to the east, Kashmir to the north, the federal routines that gave democracy a local, tangible presence were effaced, as Mrs Gandhi tried to exercise direct control over these regions.

In Punjab, during the post-Emergency years when Mrs Gandhi and the Congress were out of power, Sanjay Gandhi had set in motion a process that was to result in the Indian army's attack on the Sikh Golden Temple in June 1984, and in Mrs Gandhi's death a few months later. In order to break the power of the Sikh political party, the faction-ridden Akali Dal (which in the late 1970s was supporting the anti-Indira Gandhi government in New Delhi), Sanjay—with Mrs Gandhi's connivance—cultivated a lithe young Sikh *sant* or religious preacher, Jarnail Singh Bhindranwale.

Having helped to build him up for her own purposes, Mrs Gandhi on her return to power sought to sweep him away. But Bhindranwale would not go so gently. His militant sermons had attracted followers across the Sikh diaspora who were willing to die for him, and he committed them to an armed struggle for the creation of a Sikh homeland, Khalistan. Barricaded into the Golden Temple at Amritsar, he directed his men in a brutal campaign of terror. Finally, the Indian army launched a massive assault on the temple. Whether or not Mrs Gandhi personally commanded the use of force against this holiest of Sikh shrines remains unclear. But when her bodyguards took aim at her a few months later, they believed themselves to be very directly avenging their religion and community.

If Punjab was to prove lethal to her own person, the handling of Kashmir was to leave the country a truly poisoned legacy. Kashmir had enjoyed distinct treatment ever since its troubled accession to India in 1947: constitutionally, the state was guaranteed a standing not available to any other state in the Indian Union. Its politics had long been dominated by Nehru's friend-turned-sparring partner, Sheikh Abdullah— with whom Mrs Gandhi had made a deal, in the mid-1970s, that seemed to balance Kashmir's special autonomy with its integral place in the Indian Union.

At Sheikh Abdullah's death in 1982, his son Farooq Abdullah succeeded his father; but Mrs Gandhi never trusted him. Farooq was an unlikely leader (he was known as the 'Disco chief minister'), but he struck out on his own, refused an alliance with the Congress, and—playing on Muslim sentiment—won the elections in his state. For Mrs Gandhi, a Kashmir ruled by a leader actively resistant to her was both a personal affront and a national danger.

She was determined to oust him, and urged the governor of the state—who happened to be her cousin—to dismiss Farooq on the basis that the elections had been rigged (they were, slightly; but nothing like how they would be under Congress governments later in the 1980s). Her cousin refused and advised her against this action, so she replaced him with a more craven governor, who did the deed. The result was the build-up, during the 1980s, of a tinder pile of resentment, ready to be sparked at the very moment when de-mobbed mercenaries from the Afghan campaigns were flooding into a crisis-ridden Pakistan, and when the messages of radical Islam were radiating out from Tehran and elsewhere.

Nirad Chaudhuri, in his inimitably Indo-phobic way, once declared that, 'Not one worthy biography of a great Indian or a worthy account of Indian life or civilization has come from an Indian. That is the true *trahison des clercs* in India.' In this case, he does have a point, at least when it comes to biography. India's modern history is overpopulated with remarkable personalities, and it is a biographer's treasure trove; yet the intellectual impact made by Indian biographical writing is puny. In most cases, it is little better than hagiography or chronicle—the doings of the great, in modern recensions of the *Namas* of the Mughal emperors.

It is always hard to identify exactly what a politician has actually done: the precise nature of their responsibility for certain actions, let alone for the consequences of these actions, is maddeningly difficult to determine. The relationship between an individual politician and their deeds or acts is much less clear than that between, say, a writer and his or her literary output—a symptom of what P.N. Furbank has called 'the profound inauthenticity of the political life'. In the face of this, political biography can often fall off into a form of gossip and decorated rumour, a higher journalism. It tries to guard against this by recurring to 'sources'— documentary evidence, written or oral, that seek to clinch the link between the biographical subject and a particular act, event, or policy.

But even when available in full-text form, sources cannot really solve the problem. A biographer certainly needs to be able to determine the intentions behind a particular action or policy; but he or she needs also to grasp the relationship between the intention and the action, as well as to judge the nature of the consequences produced by the action. Only when this circuit is complete, can we get some sense of the responsibility or otherwise that a politician may bear for a particular situation. To achieve this, beyond access to sources, the biographer needs a sure interpretative grip over the political and historical field about which they are writing— a sense of the broader causalities that surround their chosen subject.

There is little doubt that Mrs Gandhi believed sincerely in what she was doing. In this utter self-conviction, she was akin to Mrs Thatcher. Both shared an obsession with national sovereignty (for Mrs Thatcher, Europe was a threat, for Mrs Gandhi, it was the world); both, in their ability to create material bases of political support, showed a consummate understanding of their political worlds (Mrs Gandhi drew the low and poor by giving them material protections, Mrs Thatcher created an electoral base for herself by creating a new class of petty property owners); and both had an outstanding ability to project their image. But sincerity and self-conviction do not explain why politicians do what they do: they precisely are part of what needs explanation.

Notes on Contributors

Bhawana Somaaya is a writer and film critic.

Ganesh N. Devy is the founder of Adivasi Academy, and is an activist campaigning for the rights of tribals and denotified communities.

Jaya Jaitly is the former chief of the Samata Party, and has conceptualized Dilli Haat in Delhi.

Leela Samson is a well-known dancer and the chief executive of Kalakshetra.

Malvika Singh is a columnist and the publisher of *Seminar* magazine.

Naazneen Karmali is a writer and consulting editor with *Business India* magazine.

Nitin Bhayana is an art collector and businessman.

Reeta Devi is a social worker.

S. Kalidas is the features editor of *India Today* magazine. He lives in New Delhi.

Sabeena Gadihoke is the author of a book on Homai Vyarawalla.

Shikha Trivedy is a features editor at NDTV.

Subhashini Ali Sahgal is the president of the All India Democratic Women's Association (AIDWA). She is also a member of the central committee of the CPI (M) in Kanpur.

Sunil Khilnani is an author. He teaches politics at Johns Hopkins University, Washington DC.

Sushila Ravindranath is the editor the *Sunday Express*. She lives in Chennai.

T.J.S. George is the author of a book on Nargis, and is a columnist with *The Sunday Express*.

Tarun J. Tejpal is an author and the editor-in-chief of *Tehelka* magazine.

Acknowledgements

It all started when Nandini Mehta, then an editor at Penguin, read an issue of *Seminar* called 'Celebrating Women'. She found it interesting and wanted me to extend the selection we had in that volume and put together this anthology. Having commissioned the book, Nandini left the company and Meru Gokhale took charge of the project. Over many a lunch at the *Seminar* office we sifted through the names of women who had been driven by an abiding passion to break new ground in their fields of work, and had broken through the confines of conservatism. She prodded me along, forcing the deadline. I thank them both for their time and involvement. To Tejbir, Jaisal and Harsh, who supported the idea, who helped make it happen, I am indebted. And, to everyone else who participated in this effort, my gratitude. Thank you all.